SUNLIGHT & BREADCRUMBS

SUNLIGHT & BREADCRUMBS

Making Food with Creativity & Curiosity

RENEE ERICKSON

with Sara Dickerman

ABRAMS, NEW YORK

To all the artists and puppies
who have passed through my life.

You slow me down and let me see the
world in all its beauty and detail.

Contents

Foreword: A Love Letter

by Jeffry Mitchell

"Raindrops on roses and whiskers on kittens, bright copper kettles . . ." What my friend Renee and I share could well be expressed in the lyrics of "My Favorite Things." It's always the little details that delight us. We met in the art studios of the University of Washington and then worked together for years at her first restaurant, Boat Street Café.

The art studio and the kitchen share so much: both kinds of work demand the everyday preparation of mise en place, the production and service, and always the cleaning up, too. In the repetition and the regularity of art making and cooking, there opens up space for the dream, the ineffable, the ethereal, and the creative.

Sharing sweet and fleeting things has sustained our friendship for decades. Sometimes they're fancy, like a martini at Bemelmans Bar at the Carlyle hotel in New York. Sometimes they are so simple, like making paper chains to decorate the Christmas tree while listening to the *Charlie Brown Christmas* album. These days we don't see each other daily, but it's not uncommon for me to get a texted photo from Renee of a new gouache painting of a cauliflower, a crab, or a quince. Or maybe a snapshot from one of her travels: a heap of artichoke from the greengrocer in Rome, a flour-dusted loaf in a wooden bakery rack, or a cute cat or puppy. (Renee is always stopping for dogs and cats.) For every creation, sharing doubles the enjoyment, like cooking a meal for family or texting a photo to a friend.

Renee's success with her restaurants, bars, and cookbooks has always been driven by her artistic intuition. This book, filled with her photographs, paintings, and divine recipes, is a testament to how those creative forces mingle in her mind. And, even better, it's an irresistible invitation for you to explore and trust your own creative impulses in the kitchen and beyond.

Jeffry Mitchell was raised in a big Catholic family in small towns across the western United States. Mitchell's grandmother taught him how to knit, crochet, quilt, and cook, and these early lessons set him on his path. He went on to study art and art history in Philadelphia and Rome and had apprenticeships in printmaking and pottery in Japan and Italy. He lives and works in Portland, Oregon, with his partner, artist Iván Carmona, and continues to make artwork that speaks to crafts domestic and decorative.

Sweet Jeffry at Boat Street Café

Introduction

Getting Back to Creative Work

I think most of us are familiar with moments of autobiographical vertigo—that dizzying feeling of "how did I get here?" from whatever moods and dreams we spent our younger days immersed in. I've had a wonderful trajectory working in food starting by running one quirky restaurant with a minimal crew to becoming a partner in a restaurant group with hundreds of employees. Though at heart I think of myself as someone who is always creating, after twenty-five years of running a business, my days are often filled with human resources meetings, check-ins with chefs and managers around town, prepping for special events, and poring over spreadsheets (so many spreadsheets!). Over the years it became easy to let my creative habits, even those that seemed so fundamental to my identity, slip by the wayside. Sitting down with a brush and paints or experimenting with a favorite ingredient became something I had to really save time for.

This book is the result of coming to grips with that gap between my perception as a creative spirit and the reality of my working life. I realized that to stay engaged with my best self, I needed to reconnect with my creative skills. That meant both painting and cooking. And, little by little, I have. Painting more and experimenting more in my home kitchen (which is also my art studio!) has energized me and helped me regain that artistic spark I've always felt. In the pages to follow, my goal is to show some of the ways I draw myself into creation in the kitchen and share some of the tools of observation, improvisation, and balance I learned in art school that help me make thoughtful and beautiful food almost every day. I needed to poke myself to get over my artistic inertia—and so, you might consider this book *your* poke to reframe your cooking as a valuable creative expression.

Why do I think it is important to focus on creativity? I have always felt most myself when I am immersed in creative work. As a child I was constantly making something, and the natural bounty of the Pacific Northwest with its moody forests, sparkling waters, and natural treasure-strewn beaches was my jumping-off point. I had sketchbooks full of chalky charcoal drawings and made a few extra dollars every

summer by painting rocks and driftwood and selling them to my neighbors and relatives.

Some people are surprised that I never went to culinary school. Instead, at the University of Washington, I majored in art. I explored many different media at studios in both Seattle and in Rome, where UW had (and still has) an outpost, just off the Campo de' Fiori. The artists I met, including teachers like Michael Spafford and Jeffry Mitchell, helped me understand the power of an artist's vision. Artists like them possess a way of observing and capturing the fragments of our experiences that others tend to overlook. They seemed so tuned in to the world, noticing the simple beauty or the chaos of life. The resulting artwork could be pretty or unsettling or puzzling, but each piece managed to hold in time a very personal response to the world we all share.

I still think about the drawing exercises Mike Spafford had my class do. He asked us to observe something—a still life, a live model. And I mean really observe—we took several minutes with this part. And then he would tell us to close our eyes and draw. He also pushed us to sketch with chunky pieces of charcoal, particularly the broad, imprecise sides of the stick. The first couple of times I wasn't thrilled with what I did— the gap between my mind and the paper was too great. But doing it over and over, you learn what this gesture or that giant smudge can do. By closing our eyes, he made it almost impossible to judge ourselves in the act of creating, which is what we are inclined to do otherwise. Mike made us immerse ourselves in experimentation, and not to pick things apart before they had a chance to become something. The confidence I have in my hands today was strengthened by that time in the studio.

Despite my studies, I didn't become a full-time artist after graduation— I bought a little restaurant instead. Painting and drawing became more infrequent as I spent late nights and early weekend mornings first at Boat Street Café and then at the many restaurants that followed. But artists, like Jeffry, Curtis Steiner, and Ellen Lesperance, have remained near and dear to me. And now, as I look back, I keep on noticing the continuum in my life between visual arts and the creativity of my life in food. At its heart, cooking, too, is a highly personal interpretation of the world around us. Each plate of food I present has a balance of color and texture and an appreciation for the negative space of the plate. When I serve food at home or at a restaurant, I try to create a relaxed and beautiful table, with flowers and candles and pretty napkins to help summon a sense of ritual. Wise and sensitive Jeffry, as he so often does, helped me put my finger on some of the many parallels between my art making and creating new recipes, in an email he sent me: "The Studio and the Kitchen are two specialized locations that house distinct pursuits and share so much." Of course, in my house, my studio *is* my kitchen. He went on: "The arc of the day, the preparation, the mise en place, the work and the finish, the cleanup, taking out the trash. The days of work structure our lives, the rhythm of work and relaxation, the marking of ordinary time and special occasions. The repetition of practice creates space for reflection, rumination, invention, and refinement. To start anew provides the chance to rethink and reconsider."

In this book, I am inviting you into my home to learn more about my creative process. I'll tap into the environment and the memories that have helped me live a creative life in food. It's my great desire that sharing reflections on my practices at home will clear new space for readers like you to savor the creative decisions we make every day. I think you will put down this book and feel ready to work in the kitchen with a little less judgment and a little more confident experimentation. You will be ready to give yourself more credit for the creative expression involved in everyday cooking.

To accomplish this, of course, recipes are the jumping off point. But you will also find essays and headnotes that connect the dots between my visual art practices and the food I cook at home and in restaurants. "Work in Progress" sidebars zoom in on the creative decisions I make when creating recipes or even just creating dinner—the seasonal ingredients, textures, shapes, and colors that help make each meal a more thoughtful expression of life at a given point in time.

Don't worry about those big ambitions, though! This is still an approachable cookbook, filled with some of my very favorite things to eat that you'll love cooking at home for quiet weeknight dinners as well as more leisurely weekend gatherings. I'll focus on how I make relatively simple food feel like a personal expression by amplifying the textures, colors, and flavors of unfussy preparations.

The food I crave most is declarative and straightforward, but it tends to feature details that make it feel distinctive. What makes it that way? In this book, I'll highlight the little, easy things that take a dish from nice to memorable.

Of course, a great meal starts with sourcing: I love to gather chicories from the farmers' market, tomatoes from my own garden, eggs from local farms, and the best seafood the Northwest has to offer, and I'll offer tips on how you can do the same, wherever you happen to call home.

When I start cooking, it's the layers of flavors and texture that bring out the most in those ingredients, and it's those details I'll offer up to home cooks in this book. Maybe it's the rich crunch of olive oil–toasted breadcrumbs on top of a hearty escarole salad or a fresh approach to pickles (page 33). You will learn to make punchy and versatile condiments like Whipped Tahini (page 38) and a spectrum of simple green sauces (page 22). Then I'll show how I tweak a great idea that's fallen out of fashion—like mushroom duxelles (page 140) or sockeye salmon with lots of mayo (page 117)—with extra chiles or citrus zest to make it sing in the present.

Vegetables are often the thing that elevates a simple meal, and many recipes will dig into all the textures that make vegetables so appealing, from an extra-crunchy slaw (page 134) to the supple, olive oil–rich texture of long-cooked zucchini (page 108).

Sometimes the distinctive detail is the setting: I love to cook and eat outside, and so I have a whole chapter on dishes that taste best in the fresh air and how to pull them off.

In these pages, you will find techniques and recipes for celebratory snacks, including beloved dips (see pages 41 and 61) and go-to crostini toppings (see pages 34 and 202). I'll conjure some of my favorite Sunday dinners, from braised beef shins (page 233) to poached halibut (page 125).

Baking is its own special ritual—I often use baking as a way to recenter myself in the kitchen after a hard workweek or a long trip. Not only do I get my hands on my favorite kitchen tools again, but having an easy dessert on hand is the perfect reason to ask a friend—or friends—over for a little catching up. You'll find recipes for some of my favorites, including my mom's brownies (page 240), an easy blackberry crostata (page 246), and a perfectly lush caramel rice pudding cake (page 265).

Presentation, from the setting to the flowers and the lighting, is always a part of the story in both my dinner parties and my cookbooks. And plating food may be the place my artistic training shows the most of all. Before I put food down on a platter, I try to think graphically, imagining the shapes and colors of each element. Take the case of a summer salad of cucumbers and melon. I imagine the bright, thick whiteness of a whipped ricotta sauce and swirl that on the base of the plate. I mix rustic chunks of cucumbers and peachy-toned melon cut in wedgelets to echo the pointed leaves of garden-plucked tarragon. These I'll pile up, not too high, not too low, making sure to reveal glimpses of the

ricotta below (negative space is always important to a composition). A few pinpricks of black pepper offset the pale summery colors of the salad; olive oil adds gloss in places. But that's enough. No need for flowers or dribbled balsamic or bigger sprigs of other herbs. Everything serves a purpose in the composition, both in terms of flavor and appearance. Learning when a dish is finished, just like any other art, is one of the trickiest, most valuable skills in the kitchen, so one entire chapter (pages 90–129) explores that idea with pared-back recipes that are special because of their simplicity.

Recently, I have noticed that I keep thinking about my creative process, the thread that connects food and art in my life. After the sorrow, stress, and isolation of the pandemic, bringing friends together (first outside, then carefully back into the house) has felt like rebuilding a world that we came close to losing. Being in my home kitchen and creating simple but memorable meals for the people I love has helped me tap back into the creative forces that have kept me going in the food industry for two and a half decades.

Creativity seems more critical to foster than ever, and this book is the result of me reflecting on what is important and what inspires me. And, in turn, the making of this very book has also drawn me deeper into the visual arts than I had been in years. In these pages, you'll find painted illustrations by me, even some ceramics here and there that I have made in my wee pottery studio. And I dove headlong into photography—I shot the photos found in these pages, extending my understanding of light, composition, and framing.

Cooking is very much about responding to and transforming the best ingredients the earth and the sea offer us and, in turn, reflecting the world around us. It's not especially distinct from making visual art, as I'm reminded in a quote the art critic Jerry Saltz recently resurfaced from Louise Bourgeois: "Art is not about art. Art is about life." In my view, that means that art-making isn't a walled-off existence but a way of living with patterns of creative habit. I'm not claiming that my family dinners are in themselves fine art, but that the practice of making them is a way to foster the same creativity that I cultivate in my painting, my design, and my photography. And so, in that spirit, I hope you enjoy sharing a bit of my creative life in these pages, and in turn find them full of prompts for how to continue exploring your own kitchen with curiosity, confidence, and an eye for detail. .

A Field Guide to Special Things

A Culinary Palette

I majored in painting at the University of Washington, and making art was part of my daily existence. Shortly after graduating in 1995, I bought a restaurant, the Boat Street Café, and as soon as I blinked, twenty-five years or so had passed, and all the painting, drawing, and shaping became something I used to do—or did very occasionally, in the company of artist friends like Jeffry Mitchell or Curtis Steiner. My home and restaurant and travels were filled with art, but art-making wasn't part of my everyday practice anymore.

Sometime in the later days of the pandemic, I committed to changing that. I bought a bunch of gouache paints. I put them on my kitchen table, in a pretty bowl, where they would greet me every morning at breakfast, a painting mise-en-place, all ready to go. And sure enough, I started to make room for painting in my life. I painted alone, I painted with my mom and dad, I painted with Jeffry and my husband, Dan. I painted Day-Glo crabs and brick-red tomatoes—it was a new way of looking at the ingredients that have inspired me in my restaurants. The art-making impulse hadn't disappeared, and it took just a little shift to get me back to it. The bowl of paint pulled me back to memories of the time I spent in the studio while studying abroad in Rome. I couldn't have known then that my creativity would largely be expressed in kitchens, but that super-focused creative work helped me realize I had a vision I wanted to share with the world.

I shouldn't have been surprised that the beckoning bowl of paint made an impact. Home cooking benefits from just the same kind of prompt. For me, cooking in my sun-streaked little kitchen always feels like a gift, a time when I can focus and linger on sensory pleasures. There are the beautiful variations of the different lettuces in my garden boxes, the rough crust of a bread loaf I'm tearing into croutons, the scent of a long-cooked braise in the oven, and the crackle of jalapeños as they char in an iron pan.

I love making meals at home, especially on a Sunday, when I'm able to cook in a leisurely way, without a clock reminding me when I need to be ready. But sometimes it's hard to get motivated to start making

things in the kitchen. That's why I try to keep the cooking equivalent of those tubes of paint close at hand: my favorite extras that make any meal a little more special. These culinary prompts are a little more than just pantry favorites. These elements help make an ordinary middle-of-the week meal into something worth lingering over. They add freshness, salt, complexity, or texture. In short, they add *delight* to the relatively straightforward dishes I cook at home. A few examples: breadcrumbs—not just packaged breadcrumbs but shatteringly crisp mini-croutons toasted on the stovetop in plenty of olive oil—can elevate a quick summer meal of grilled vegetables. Oven-dried tomatoes only need a piece of crunchy toast and some whipped ricotta to get me dreaming about sunny Lazio in the middle of the winter.

Again and again, I return to the things in this chapter: they are the reliable, transformative components to meals that always make me feel like rolling up my sleeves and getting started. These elements bring me back to the joy of creating that's shared in my cooking and my artwork alike. I can't wait to share them with you.

A Note on Some of My Favorite Basics

Throughout the book, there are some basics so integral to my cooking that I may not remember to be very specific in individual recipes. Salt is one of my favorite things. When I call for just "salt" in a recipe, I am referring to my own practice of grinding some sea salt in a mortar and pestle to a texture that's a bit rougher than fine sea salt, and finer than kosher salt. I like the textural control I get from this easy, satisfying process. If I call for "flaky salt," I am thinking of a texturally interesting finishing salt, and most often at home I use Maldon.

Olive oil for me is always extra-virgin: I usually use Moroccan olive oil for cooking and general use, and then an assortment of more expensive estate-grown Italian oils for a spicy finishing touch (I'll often call those "fancy").

Citrus juice and peels are mainstays for me and should always be squeezed or zested right before using.

The same goes for ground black pepper, which I rarely measure because I just grind it into the dish.

Mayonnaise is also a favorite ingredient. Homemade is always delicious, but Best Foods/Hellmann's is consistently good, and I use it all the time in my cooking.

Resources for Specialty Ingredients

FLOUR
Cairnspring Mills, www.cairnspring.com

If you have a mill that focuses on local and heritage grains, by all means choose something local, but I rely on this Burlington, Washington, mill for most of my baking projects.

HAZELNUTS
Holmquist Hazelnut Orchards, www.holmquisthazelnuts.com

HUCKLEBERRIES AND LOVELY MUSHROOMS
Foraged and Found Edibles, www.foragedandfoundedibles.com

OYSTERS AND MANILA CLAMS
Hama Hama Oyster Company, www.hamahamaoysters.com

DUNGENESS CRAB AND SMOKED BLACK COD AND SALMON
Pike Place Fish Market via Goldbelly, www.goldbelly.com

SPICES AND TAHINI
Villa Jerada, www.villajerada.com

THERMOMETER
Lavatools Pro Duo. www.lavatools.co

Having a reliable, easy-to-read digital thermometer is a surprisingly wonderful kitchen upgrade. I don't know why it took me so long to get a nice one.

VINEGARS, HOT SAUCES, OLIVE OILS, ANCHOVIES, BOTTARGA, AND HARD-TO-FIND CONDIMENTS
ChefShop, www.chefshop.com

Delaurenti, www.delaurenti.com

WILD SALMON—FLASH FROZEN AT SEA AND SHIPPED TO YOUR HOME—A GREAT RESOURCE, ESPECIALLY IF YOU LIVE FAR FROM THE OCEAN
Drifters Fish, www.driftersfish.com (also for spot prawns in season)

Eva's Wild, www.evaswild.com

One—OK, Maybe Two or Three— Green Sauces, Used Over and Over

Green sauce is one of the great tools in my kit: It brings brightness, acid, and, not insignificantly, lovely color to the plate. Best of all, green sauces don't take a lot of premeditation to assemble, especially in the summer when the garden boxes in my alley are filled with herbs. Green sauces are essential all around the globe from Argentina to India, Italy to Mexico. I started this book with one green sauce, and then had to add another and another! Here is one with a big handful of chives— great to pair with seafood or fresh cheeses—and another with a little chile kick that's perfect for grilled chicken or steak, and another that is powered with ginger. As you get to know your green sauces, you can tweak the balance of herbs (basil, cilantro, and other tender green herbs work nicely), acids (lemon juice, vinegar), and extras like capers and anchovies. Leftover green sauce of any variation can be stored in an airtight jar in the refrigerator for up to two days. It will stay fresher if the herbs are covered with olive oil, so add a bit extra if necessary. And when you use refrigerated green sauce, taste and add a bit of citrus juice to liven it up if necessary. One option for a slightly older jar of green sauce is to use it as a marinade.

Chive-Dill Green Sauce

Makes about 1½ cups (360 ml)

This densely dark green sauce would be a deliciously aromatic take on a potato salad dressing, or tasty stirred into cream cheese for a brunch spread.

1 shallot, minced

¼ cup (11 g) minced chives

½ cup (13 g) minced dill

½ cup (25 g) minced Italian parsley

½ cup (120 ml) olive oil

½ teaspoon salt, plus more as needed

2 tablespoons lemon juice

In a medium bowl, mix all the ingredients together. Check for seasoning.

Jalapeño Green Sauce

Makes about 1½ cups (360 ml)

This sauce has a mellow spiciness that could make a lively marinade for a simple pork chop or add a bit of charisma to a nice batch of deviled eggs. I like to chop the parsley, garlic, capers, and jalapeño all together (and very finely) to really meld their flavors.

1 heaping cup (75 g) Italian parsley leaves, very finely chopped

2 cloves garlic, minced

1 tablespoon capers, minced

1 whole jalapeño chile, seeded if you like it less spicy, very finely chopped

2 anchovy fillets, minced

Pinch of red chile flakes

Grated zest and juice of 1 lime

¾ cup (180 ml) olive oil

Salt and freshly ground black pepper

In a medium bowl, combine the parsley, garlic, capers, chile, and anchovy fillets. Stir in the chile flakes, lime zest and juice, and olive oil. Stir well, taste, and adjust the seasoning with salt and pepper.

Ginger Green Sauce

Makes about ¾ cup (180 ml)

I make this sauce almost weekly—it's part of the ginger renaissance in my home. I love it over rice dishes, grilled meats, and most often with roasted vegetables and Whipped Tahini (page 38).

½ cup (120 ml) olive oil, plus more as needed

Grated zest and juice of 1 lime

3 cloves garlic, grated

¼ cup each (13 g) minced fresh Italian parsley, mint, and cilantro

3-inch (7.5 cm) piece fresh ginger, peeled and grated

1 serrano chile, seeds removed, minced

Pinch of Aleppo pepper

Salt

Place all the ingredients in a medium bowl and stir to combine. Add more olive oil if you want it a bit looser.

Pangrattato, Above-Average Breadcrumbs

Makes about 1½ cups (150 g)

Good bread makes for great breadcrumbs. It's all part of the natural order of the kitchen. I just love well-seasoned ones like these: a variation on the Italian toasted breadcrumbs called pangrattato. Once you have made them, you won't be able to stop sprinkling them about. I love these twirled with pasta in anchovy-chile oil and on top of steamed clams. Oh, and to finish soft scrambled eggs in the morning, and on top of my meat loaf. I could go on and on.

3 packed cups (300 g) stale bread, torn into big chunks

½ cup (120 ml) olive oil

2 cloves garlic, peeled

1 teaspoon salt

In a food processor, pulse the bread several times to break it down into crumbs. Heat a large (at least 10 inches/25 cm) skillet over medium-high heat. Add half the olive oil and 1 clove garlic, toast the garlic for 1 minute, then add half the breadcrumbs and salt. Toast the crumbs in the oil for 3 to 4 minutes, stirring frequently, removing and discarding the garlic after about 1 minute.

When the crumbs are dark golden brown, remove them to a plate to cool. Repeat the process with the remaining bread, oil, garlic, and salt.

If you want the cool crumbs a bit finer, pulse them in the food processor again for a quick second.

These will keep in an airtight container at room temperature for about 3 days. If they have sat around a bit, feel free to re-toast them for a few minutes to crisp them up.

Variation: Plain Dried Breadcrumbs

Breadcrumbs to be used in cooked dishes like meatballs and meat loaf can be prepared with a leaner, drier method. Wait until bread is a few days old and getting a little dry, then slice or tear it into chunks (I generally keep the crust on for this). Cook in a preheated 350°F (175°C) oven in an uncrowded layer on a sheet pan, turning the pieces from time to time, until they are dry all the way through and ever so lightly browned. Let cool, then pulse the bread chunks in a food processor until they are coarsely crumbly. Store in an airtight container in a dry spot for a week or for several months in the freezer.

Oven-Dried Tomatoes

Makes about 5 cups (380 g)

One of the easiest ways to preserve summer tomatoes at their peak is to slowly dry them in the oven, pop them into a jar, cover them with good olive oil, and keep them stored in the fridge for a cold winter day. They are a real gift in January when you are dreaming of summer. If you are desperate, you can do this with hothouse-grown Roma tomatoes, but they will not be as good as summer tomatoes—although drying will improve the flavor of a winter tomato immensely.

2 pounds (900 g) small Roma or datterini tomatoes

¼ cup (60 ml) olive oil, plus more for packing

Salt

Preheat the oven to 200°F (95°C).

Wash the tomatoes and slice them in half from stem to tail. Place them in a large bowl. Pour the olive oil over them, season well with salt, and give them a good toss. Lay the tomatoes out on two wire cooling racks, each set upon a baking sheet, with the cut side facing up. Drizzle them with the olive oil left in the bowl. Place in the oven and bake until dried but still pliable, 3 to 4 hours. Let cool.

Place the dried tomatoes in 2 or 3 sterile glass pint (480 ml) jars and cover with more olive oil. These can be stored in the fridge for up to 3 months (or frozen for longer, if you store them in plastic rather than glass). As you pull tomatoes from the container, make sure you always cover the remaining ones with more oil, if needed.

Charred Then Pickled Jalapeños and Onions

Makes 8 cups (1.9 liters)

After years of pickling, you would think there was nothing more to learn, but I keep on experimenting. Having cooked a lot of Mexican-inspired food for the past few years, I decided to incorporate the classic first step of many salsas, blistering ingredients in a hot pan, into my pickle process. Charring the peppers and onions gives a bit of smoky flavor and makes the resulting pickle less "green" and more savory. These pickles aren't overwhelmingly hot, especially if you don't use the seeds. They are delicious in a sauce for grilled fish or chicken, slivered as an accent for raw tuna tartare, or, not surprisingly, as a component of a great pico de gallo for chips. And think about chopping a little onion and pepper from this jar to mix in your next potato salad (page 162) or tuna melt (page 94).

1 pound (455 g) jalapeño chiles

1 large white onion (about 8 ounces/ 225 g), peeled and quartered

2 cups (480 ml) white wine vinegar

2 tablespoons toasted coriander seeds

1 tablespoon toasted cumin seeds

5 cloves garlic, peeled

2 tablespoons sugar

1 teaspoon sea salt

Sterilize a 2-quart (1.9 liter) canning jar and its lid (or use two smaller jars). Heat a heavy skillet over high heat—I like a cast-iron one. Place some of the chiles into the pan, making sure not to crowd them. Cook until charred on one side and then turn to char another surface until all sides of the chile are charred, a total of about 10 minutes. Repeat with the rest of the chiles.

Place the onion quarters in the hot pan and char them on each cut side, about 2 minutes per side.

Place 2 cups (480 ml) water, the vinegar, coriander seeds, cumin seeds, garlic, sugar, and salt in a medium nonreactive pot. Add the charred chiles and onion quarters. Bring to a boil over high heat, then lower the heat and simmer for 12 minutes.

Put the big chunks in the jar first, then pour over the brine, making sure the brine covers the chunks. Cover and let cool to room temperature, then place in the refrigerator. They will keep for about 2 months in the fridge.

Whipped Feta

Makes 2 cups (480 ml)

This is just such an easy technique to make a little dip that stands in pretty swoops and folds onto a piece of toasted bread for easy crostini, or beneath a pile of oven-roasted tomatoes. I make it with two fresh cheeses: feta and ricotta. If you choose feta, find a version with sheep's milk in it: I like Fleecemaker from Bow, Washington, but Valbreso from France is good too. Sheep feta has a softer aspect than goat-milk feta, something I love in this preparation. If you use ricotta, make sure to work with a smaller-batch variety of whole-milk ricotta like Bellwether or Calabro hand-dipped ricotta. Soaked in brine, feta is generally salty enough, so it doesn't usually need much seasoning after being whipped, but ricotta may need a boost of salt. P.S.: These are universally great spreads for vegetarian sandwiches—coat both cut sides of a baguette with the whipped cheese and layer in cucumbers, peppers (raw or roasted), tender greens, grilled mushrooms, fresh or roasted tomatoes, you name it.

8 ounces (225 g) feta cheese in a block, not crumbled

¼ cup (60 ml) plain whole-milk yogurt

Grated zest of ½ lemon

2 tablespoons olive oil, plus more for drizzling

Edible flower petals (optional)

Combine the cheese, yogurt, and lemon zest in a food processor fitted with a steel blade and start spinning the mixture. As the machine runs, drizzle in the olive oil through the hole in the lid. Whip on high until very smooth, about 90 seconds. Scrape into a bowl and chill for at least 30 minutes; it will firm up a bit. It will keep in an airtight container in the fridge for 2 days. To serve, drizzle with olive oil and sprinkle with the edible flower petals, if using.

Variation: Whipped Ricotta

Substitute 12 ounces (340 g) whole-milk ricotta (like Bellwether) for the feta and omit the yogurt from the recipe. Process the same way as above, and season with salt and freshly cracked black pepper to taste at the end.

Canning tomatoes with Mom

A stack of sesame flatbread

Caviar & oyster party

Whipped Tahini

Makes 3 cups (720 ml)

Tahini needs just a nudge to make it into a plush sauce to dress up a whole stable of dishes. It's just the thing if you've roasted a chicken, or if your grilled vegetables need a little something else. And it can also be a complement to a more acidic sauce: you could pair it with one of the green sauces from page 22, for example, to dress up a plate of grilled sardines. Do look for a high-quality tahini from a source with good turnover, because the sesame paste is so front and center in this sauce. I like my friend Medhi's Villa Jerada tahini, as well as Soom.

1 clove garlic, roughly chopped, plus more as needed

Juice of 1 lemon (about ⅓ cup/75 ml), plus more as needed

1 pound (455 g) tahini

1 tablespoon toasted and ground cumin, plus more as needed

1 tablespoon salt, plus more as needed

1½ cups (360 ml) ice-cold water

In a food processor fitted with a steel blade, buzz the garlic and lemon juice in pulses until well blended, about 1 minute total, pausing to scrape down the garlic if it sticks to the walls. Let the garlicky juice sit for 10 minutes for the garlic to mellow out.

Add the tahini and process for 1 to 2 minutes, until it thickens, occasionally stopping to scrape down the sides.

Add the cumin and salt, and with the motor running, slowly drizzle in the cold water through the hole in the lid until the sauce flows smoothly and turns to a creamy white color. Don't worry: The mixture usually looks rough and bumpy before it smooths back out.

Check the seasoning—you can tune your tahini with more garlic, lemon, cumin, salt, and olive oil to taste.

Store for up to 5 days in an airtight container in the fridge. After refrigerating, you can brighten up the flavor of the whipped tahini with a squeeze of lemon before serving.

Caviar Dip for a Party

Serves 6 to 8

Caviar is a self-proclaimed special ingredient. And it is so good: the kind of mini-indulgence that makes a party. A little caviar goes a long way in this delicious dip, a blend of mascarpone cheese, sour cream, and a swirl of green sauce. Don't forget the potato chips. If you don't love caviar already, this will for sure turn you around. A friend brought a fun and fancy dip like this to a dinner, and I've been making my own variations ever since.

With no need for bone spoons, blinis, or iced silver bowls, this is a playful way to serve caviar of any kind, from precious Osetra to easy-to-find salmon roe (ikura). The recipe makes a generous portion, but it will go quickly when your guests arrive. I love this on New Year's Eve.

1 pound (455 g) sour cream

½ cup (120 ml) mascarpone cheese

1 clove garlic, finely grated on a Microplane

1 teaspoon sea salt

1 batch Chive-Dill Green Sauce (page 22), plus a few extra chopped chives, if you have them

1¾ ounces (47 g) fancy caviar or your preferred fish eggs

Plenty of your favorite plain potato chips

In a stand mixer fitted with a paddle attachment, combine the sour cream, mascarpone, garlic, and salt. Mix on low speed until there are no lumps. Cover with plastic wrap and set in the fridge until ready to serve (up to 1 day ahead of serving).

When ready to serve, scoop the sour cream mixture into a low bowl. Using the back of a spoon, make a well in the middle of the mixture, banking it up a little on the side of the bowl. Pour the green sauce into the well, so you have a circle of green surrounded by the ring of white. Top both areas with generous spoonfuls of the caviar. I like to create small piles of caviar all over the top of the dip—have fun with this one. You can also split it into two dishes so you can bring a second one out later for the fashionably late folks. Just before serving, sprinkle with a few extra chopped chives, if you have them, and serve with potato chips.

Go-To Vinaigrette

Makes about ⅓ cup (75 ml)

Delicious vinegars are a sure way to turn up the intrigue in everyday cooking, and my favorite kind tends to shift over time—there are so many delicious options, from sherry to Banyuls to red wine vinegar (for the latter, it is so worth seeking out great brands like Volpaia or Pojer e Sandri—order online! It's easy, and trust me, they are worth it!). Lately, I'm even taking it back to the nineties and really enjoying balsamic vinegar, like the one made by Cleto Chiarli, with its concentrated sweetness, which I whisk into a vinaigrette offset with a good dollop of sharp mustard. Note this recipe only makes a bit, because vinaigrette is truly tastiest if you make it just before mixing it with your salad. I usually make it in the bottom of my salad bowl, and then toss the greens right in with it. Feel free to sub out the balsamic for a well-made white or red wine vinegar. And you'll see that this is one of those flexible recipes. Why? Because the vinegar is going to dictate how much oil is desirable in relation to it. Very fine vinegars tend to be less astringent than grocery store ones, and thus need less olive oil to soften their blow. That, and I like a puckery vinaigrette, and you might like it softer. So, start with this ratio, and whisk in more oil to get the balance you like.

3 tablespoons good vinegar: artisanal balsamic, sherry, red or white wine, plus more as needed

Salt

1 teaspoon Dijon mustard

¼ cup (60 ml) or more olive oil (one on the buttery side: with a charismatic vinegar you don't need to use an aggressive olive oil)

Freshly ground black pepper

Start with the vinegar in the bowl you plan to mix your salad in, then whisk in a couple pinches of salt. Whisk in the mustard, then whisk briskly while slowly streaming in the olive oil; the dressing will thicken a bit as the oil gets incorporated. Grind in a good bit of black pepper. Dip a little lettuce leaf in and taste the dressing. Adjust the seasoning if needed, and if it's too sharp, add a bit more oil, or if it needs a bit more punch, stir in some more vinegar.

Painting party with Mom & Dad

Sunny path to the beach

Pearly Everlasting,
a local wildflower

Aioli for Every Occasion

Makes about 1⅔ cups (405 ml)

Whenever your grilled fish is a little drab, or your sandwich is a little dry, or your French fries need a little something new to dip into, you can count on aioli, garlicky homemade mayonnaise. It's just the best. And if you have an immersion blender, you can use it to make your aioli; work in a narrow round-sided jar, and you'll be able to store your mayo without transferring it to a different container!

1 large egg yolk

½ teaspoon Dijon mustard

2 teaspoons lemon juice

½ cup (120 ml) neutral oil, like grapeseed or canola

½ cup (120 ml) olive oil

2 cloves garlic, grated

Salt

In a food processor fitted with a metal blade, combine the egg yolk, mustard, 1 teaspoon water, and the lemon juice. Turn the machine on to combine, then slowly drizzle in the neutral and olive oils. Once the sauce is thick and emulsified, add the garlic and salt to taste; if the mayo seems too gloppy and thick, then you can add a teaspoon of hot water at a time to thin it out.

Note: The garlic taste grows stronger as time goes on, so feel free to add another clove of garlic if serving right away, or a bit less if serving later. This can be made up to 1 day in advance; store in an airtight jar in the refrigerator.

Warm Marinated Olives

Serves 8 to 10

I always think I'll be ready when guests arrive, but then then there's that one little thing I forgot to do earlier—maybe light the grill or grab greens from the garden. And suddenly I'm not so ready after all. That's where olives—OK, potato chips and cold rosé too—come in handy: something decadent and delicious that is ready to go the moment people walk in the door. A few tips to make olives special: It's nice to have several kinds. Some of my favorites include Castelvetrano, Cerignola, salt-cured black olives (like Niçoise), and some juicy black olives like Kalamata or Taggiasca. Olives with their pits intact are more delicious—they keep their individual character more than hollowed-out olives, which get more heavily brined. And do go through the extra step of warming your olives: It will make all the flavors—the citrus, garlic, and spices—in this recipe come alive.

½ cup (120 ml) olive oil

2 cloves garlic, thinly sliced

Zest of 1 lemon, cut into thin strips

½ teaspoon chopped rosemary

2 fresh bay leaves

½ teaspoon fennel seeds

2 tablespoons good red wine vinegar (see recommended brands, page 42)

2 cups (360 g) mixed olives, drained, with pits intact

Preheat the oven to 350°F (175°C)—or you can warm the olives on the grill if you have that going.

Pour the olive oil into a low heatproof dish. Add the garlic, lemon zest, rosemary, bay leaves, fennel seeds, and vinegar and whisk well.

Stir in the olives and place the dish in the oven. Heat just until the oil is fragrant and the olives are warmed through: 7 to 10 minutes, depending on how cold they are to start. Serve.

The marinated olives can be kept in an airtight jar in the refrigerator for a couple weeks. Just warm up to room temperature before serving.

Grilled Sesame Flatbread

Makes twelve 6- to 7-inch (15 to 17 cm) round flatbreads

I use plenty of grilled bread and toasted baguettes in my kitchen, but sometimes I feel like making a special bit of flatbread to tear and dip into an extra-savory broth (see beef shin, page 233), sop up a delicious salad dressing (like the one in the CSA Slaw, page 134), or top with cheese (see Spicy Marinated Feta, page 170). This sesame flatbread is closely inspired by the *Honey & Co.* pita recipe—I love everything Sarit and Itamar do. You could bake it on a stone in a 400°F (205°C) oven, but the char from the grill is a special summery delight.

¼ cup (40 g) sesame seeds

2 teaspoons fast-acting or instant yeast

1 tablespoon sugar

About 1¾ cups (420 ml) lukewarm water

6 cups (750 g) all-purpose flour, plus more for dusting

¼ cup (30 g) milk powder

2 teaspoons salt

2 tablespoons olive oil, plus more for the bowl and cooking

Toast the sesame seeds in a dry skillet over medium-high heat, stirring frequently, until lightly browned, about 1 minute. Remove from the pan and cool.

In a small bowl, combine the yeast, sugar, and ¾ cup plus 2 tablespoons (210 ml) of the lukewarm water. Stir to combine. After a few minutes, check to make sure the mixture is bubbling a bit.

Put the flour, milk powder, and salt in the bowl of a stand mixer fitted with a dough hook. Mix on low speed to combine, about 30 seconds. Turn the speed up to medium and gradually pour in the yeast mixture. Continue processing and add the olive oil. Process for 30 more seconds and then add the sesame seeds. Keep the machine running; it will look messy and clumpy at first. While it combines, add the remaining water a bit at a time. You may need to stop the machine occasionally and push the dough down in the early stages. Let the machine run until the dough comes together as a smooth elastic ball.

Transfer the dough to a clean, lightly oiled bowl. Cover the bowl with plastic wrap and let sit in a warm place for about 1 hour.

About 30 to 40 minutes before cooking, prepare a grill to medium-high heat, spreading the coals out pretty evenly across the grill once the flames die down. Divide the dough into 12 even pieces, just under 4 ounces (115 g) each. Roll each piece into a smooth ball. Place each ball onto a floured sheet pan and cover with plastic. Let the dough rest for 10 minutes.

Flour a clean surface and have two lightly floured baking sheets ready. Take one of the dough balls and smoosh it into a flattened circle. Using a rolling pin, roll the dough into a circle 6 to 7 inches (15 to 20 cm) across. Lay the dough circle on a lightly floured sheet pan. Repeat with the remaining dough balls, dusting each circle lightly with flour and overlapping slightly to fit 6 pieces on each tray. Cover each tray with plastic wrap or a slightly damp kitchen towel. Let rise for 20 minutes.

When the grate is hot, clean it well with a grill brush and rub a bit of olive oil on it, using a pair of tongs and a paper towel lightly drizzled with olive oil. Lay 3 dough rounds on the hot grate. Cook for 2 minutes untouched, letting the bread bubble up. Drizzle the top of each bread with a bit of olive oil. Flip the bread and cook until browned on the second side, rotating every 20 seconds or so to make sure it cooks evenly. When golden brown on both sides, remove to a platter and repeat with the remaining dough circles. Place the finished breads beneath a clean kitchen towel while cooking the rest of the flatbreads and serve while warm.

Parmigiano-Reggiano Broth

Makes 7½ cups (1.8 liters)

Parmigiano-Reggiano is like oxygen in my kitchen—completely essential and omnipresent. And so, I end up with a lot of Parmesan rinds. I store them in a little container in the freezer, and when I have enough, I make a batch of Parmigiano-Reggiano Broth. On a winter day when you need some soothing, cook up a bit of tiny pastina in the Parm broth and slurp it up with more Parm and a good glug of spicy olive oil. Parm broth is also the perfect boost to almost any soup or batch of beans—you can see one way I use it in my recipe for beans on toast (page 81).

6 to 10 pieces (about 8 ounces/ 225 g) dried Parmigiano-Reggiano cheese rind

Place the rinds in large stockpot with 2 quarts (2 liters) water. Bring to a boil, then reduce the heat to maintain a gentle simmer. Partially cover and cook for 2 hours, then strain. Cool, then store the broth in an airtight container in the refrigerator for up to 5 days or in the freezer for up to 3 months.

Anchovies Make (Almost) Everything Better

Tinned Excellence

A key focus of this book is how thoughtful details can push a creative project, even just a simple dinner, into extra-special territory. To illustrate this, I wanted to zoom in on one of my favorite cooking elements—the small and mighty anchovy. The anchovy is an anchor in my kitchen. I love that its plain appearance can so easily build up the savory resonance of a dish.

Anchovies are one small fish, several species of the family *Engraulidae*, and unless you are fishing with live bait, you are most likely to find them preserved with salt and oil. When I was growing up in Woodinville, Washington, in the eighties, anchovies were shorthand for something gross. Like, *Who would put anchovies on a pizza?* It's the kind of thing a teacher would bring up to a classroom of kids just to get them to squeal "EEEEEWWWW!" I'm sure that pop-culture joking about anchovies had a lingering bit of anti-immigrant stereotyping about it, because it was southern Mediterranean immigrants to the US, most notably from Italy, who used the little salty fish to bring mysterious beauty to so many dishes. If anchovies were hanging around less food-centric households, they were likely mushed up in a tube of anchovy paste so no one had to confront their fishy origins. Little did I know as a kid that some of my favorite flavors, like lush, herby green goddess dip (page 61)—got that little something extra from anchovies.

Salty little fish have a long history of being coveted. The Greeks and Romans would process them to make various fermented fish elixirs including garum, which concentrated the glutamates—aka umami molecules—into a potent condiment to deliver both salt and richness to meals. Like balsamic vinegar today, there was a range of quality in garum: Noble families could enjoy a thick, more concentrated liquid, while institutional cooks would lean on a more dilute fish sauce. Today, you can find the modern Italian version of garum made from anchovies and sold as colatura. Of course, salty little fish aren't just a Western phenomenon; they also have a long history in Asian cuisines, and many

of my favorite Thai and Vietnamese dishes get their little something special from fermented fish sauce.

I think another reason many Americans took a while to come around to the joy of anchovies is quality—the cans you might grab at the grocery when you run out are just not that lovely—they are often small, ragged, and unsubtly salty. It's best to seek out Italian or Spanish anchovy imports, and the colorful graphics on the cans' labels are almost worth the purchase alone. True devotees often gravitate to whole salt-packed anchovies, like those I wondered about in Rome. They are the largest and the lushest preserved anchovies around—the Agostino Recca brand is a classic that's sold in specialty delis everywhere. When you are ready to use them, you rinse the salt off and soak them for 15 minutes or so. You then pull off the fillets from the fish skeleton and use them as is or marinate them in olive oil with herbs and garlic if you like. These are undeniably scrumptious, but if the rinsing and soaking slows down your anchovy inclination—don't sweat it. There are plenty of beautiful oil-packed filleted anchovies to enjoy. Good brands like Ortiz, Donostia, El Capricho, and Scalia offer broad, sleek anchovies. One note on handling anchovies: If they have been refrigerated, make sure to let them come to room temperature before using—this will let the olive oil re-liquify and keep them from breaking as you pull them out of the jar.

I started becoming more anchovy conscious when I first went to Rome. I would go into the alimentari—specialty food stores—to gape at the beautiful cheeses and salumi. There I would see giant cans of neatly arranged salted anchovies. *How could they sell all those little fish?* I wondered. I didn't really start using them in my own cooking until Boat Street Café, the restaurant I would eventually own. Owner Susan Kaplan had traveled extensively in France and thought that Seattle diners were ready to get over their anchovy phobia. Her menus featured anchovy-laced salad Niçoise and anchovy mayonnaise. I finally understood what all the fuss was about. There was an intensity and persistence to the anchovy flavor that was startling to me. At the same time, anchovies could be subtle: They melt into a mirepoix at the beginning of a braise or blend invisibly into a dressing. The shadow of the anchovies would then be there, adding a savory insistence without actually seeming "fishy."

One of the great things about being well-stocked in anchovies is there is a full spectrum of anchovy intensity to enjoy: They can bring background notes to a sauce or a pasta dish or take the spotlight on, yes, a pizza. Other times, I like to show them off: I think they are quite elegant. I can draw a strict little line across a wedge of toast with one and drape others in a salad like glossy little ribbons.

Over time, you begin to recognize patterns in the ways you create. When I paint with gouache, I like to lay down my color in bold, kind of smooshy brushstrokes. It's a throughline in my work even as the subjects and scale change. Style evolves with repeated practice—your gestures are no longer something you are actively thinking about. Anchovies play a similar role in my cooking: a way for me to tune a dish to really feel like mine.

Enjoy the recipes in this chapter: They show just how versatile anchovies are, and how they can please fish lovers and anchovy skeptics alike in their various guises. I think you'll begin to understand why they are my favorite of favorite things.

Easiest Anchovies

Before we get to the recipes, here are five things you can do with anchovies, almost without thinking.

1. Make a platter with fancy anchovies, butter, a jar of Dijon, and a sleeve of saltines.

2. Spread a slice of good bread with both olive oil and butter, lay down a super thin slice of lemon, and top with your best anchovies.

3. Another saltine idea: Butter the crackers and top with spicy IASA anchovies in an oil-based chile relish.

4. Make Gildas for a party: Wrap an anchovy around a pitted green olive like a Gordal or Castelvetrano, skewer it with a toothpick, and add a single piparra pepper on the end.

5. And easiest of all, open a can of Spanish anchovy-stuffed olives, drain it, and put them in a bowl with some olive oil. They are so good and the perfect cocktail garnish!

Marinated Leg of Lamb

My favorite anchovies

Green goddess & Summer Vegetables

Green Goddess Dip with Salmon Eggs and Radishes

Serves 6 to 8

Green goddess—it's totally worthy of worship. It has everything that I love: So many herbs. Hidden anchovies. Mayonnaise. Vivid color. It's just so good—and that same delicious salad dressing can also be showcased as a dip: it just depends on how you present it. In this version, I push the greenness of the dip by quickly blanching the herbs before blending. And then, to make the whole thing extra-special, I dab coral salmon roe on top of the green and pre-dip some radishes with their ruffled leaves into the bowl. If you serve it like I do, your guests may find it easier to scoop a big spoonful onto a plate and then dip their chips from there (or you can keep the radishes on the side).

½ teaspoon salt, plus more as needed and to blanch the herbs

2 cups (80 g) basil leaves

1 cup (60 g) Italian parsley leaves

¾ cup (45 g) tarragon leaves

2 tablespoons lemon juice, plus more as needed

1 cup (240 ml) mayonnaise

1 cup (240 ml) crème fraîche

4 anchovy fillets

1 clove garlic, minced

3 tablespoons olive oil

1 bunch radishes, leaves intact, sliced into halves and some quarters

1 (2-ounce/60 g) jar salmon eggs

1 bag good potato chips (I like Kettle Chips)

Prepare a bath of icy water in a bowl. Bring a medium pot of salted water to a boil. Place the basil leaves into the water, pushing them down to immerse. As soon as they soften, lift them out of the water with a slotted spoon and place them in the ice water. Repeat the process with the parsley and tarragon leaves. Drain the chilled herbs, pulling out any remaining ice, squeeze the excess water out, and roughly chop them.

Combine the chopped blanched herbs, lemon juice, salt, mayonnaise, crème fraîche, anchovies, garlic, and olive oil in a blender or food processor and pulse until very smooth. Taste the dressing and adjust with salt and/or lemon juice if desired. Place the green goddess in the fridge until ready to serve; green goddess tastes best served within a day of making.

At serving time, pour the dip into a wide shallow serving bowl and lay the radishes across the top of the dip. Spoon little clusters of the salmon eggs onto the radishes. Serve with potato chips.

Lemon, Anchovy, and Caper Compound Butter

Makes about 1 cup (225 g) butter

I love citrus peels—grated on a Microplane or ribboned with a peeler before slicing into long, thin julienne strips. I put them in almost all marinades, green sauces, stuff them into a chicken cavity before I roast it, and my favorite, add them to shellfish when steaming. But what complements lemon zest better than anchovies? I like to mash them together in a compound butter that effectively serves as ready-to-go sauce to lift your favorite simple preparations into newly delicious territory. Melt the butter, and you are ready to dress up vegetables, grilled meat, roasted chicken, or pan-sautéed fish. Or dab it on oysters before grilling them (page 178). The flavored butter is freezable, so you can have something on hand for last-minute options. The basic flavored butter technique is one I use again and again: I make compound butters with fermented chile sauce, seaweed flakes, or finely processed garlic scapes (see variation).

1 cup (2 sticks/225 g) unsalted butter, softened

2 tablespoons capers, chopped

Finely grated zest of 1 lemon (use a Microplane)

6 anchovy fillets, chopped and then smashed into a paste with the side of the knife

1 tablespoon lemon juice

In a stand mixer with the paddle attachment, beat the butter on medium speed for 15 seconds. Add the capers, lemon zest, anchovies, and lemon juice. Beat for 1 minute, or until all the ingredients are well incorporated.

If not using right away, you can roll the butter into a cylinder using parchment paper. If you won't use that within a couple of weeks, then wrap the parchment tube well in plastic wrap and freeze for up to 3 months. You can slice off the amount you need to use as you go along.

Variation: Garlic Scape, Anchovy, and Parsley Butter

Garlic scapes (stalks) make a brief spring appearance in the markets and are wonderful for adding an herbaceous garlic punch to a versatile butter. This variation yields about 1½ cups (340 g).

1 cup (2 sticks/225 g) unsalted butter, softened, plus 2 additional tablespoons

10 garlic scapes, woody ends trimmed, chopped into ½-inch (12 mm) pieces (if not available, you can substitute 10 spring garlic cloves)

1 cup (50 g) roughly chopped Italian parsley leaves

Grated zest of 1 lemon

6 anchovy fillets, chopped

⅓ cup (75 ml) lemon juice, about 2 lemons

1 teaspoon salt

In a medium skillet, melt the 2 tablespoons butter over medium-low heat. Add the garlic scapes and sauté until tender, 3 to 4 minutes. Scrape the scapes and their pan juices into a blender while warm. Add the parsley and buzz them together until smooth.

In a stand mixer fitted with paddle attachment, beat the remaining 1 cup (2 sticks/225 g) butter on medium speed for 15 seconds. Add the blended scapes, lemon zest, anchovies, lemon juice, and salt. Beat for 1 minute, or until all the ingredients are well incorporated.

Store in the same manner as the compound butter above.

Escarole Caesar with Creamy Anchovy Dressing, Parmigiano, and Pangrattato

Serves 4 to 6

Sometimes small themes and variations are the best way to explore the potential of a classic dish like Caesar salad. I love Caesar dressing, but I have no real desire to make it with romaine again—I love using the dressing on more charismatic crunchy greens, from radicchio to lacinato kale to another favorite, juicy escarole. I made one additional textural twist too—a generous sprinkling of pan-toasted breadcrumbs instead of big chunky croutons—it's a way to get a better crunch-to-bite ratio in your salad.

1 clove garlic, peeled

Salt

6 oil-cured anchovies

5 teaspoons lemon juice, plus more as needed

¾ teaspoon Worcestershire sauce

1 teaspoon balsamic vinegar

Freshly ground black pepper

1 large egg yolk

¾ cup (180 ml) mild olive oil

1 medium head escarole (about 12 ounces (340 g), leaves separated and torn into reasonable pieces

1 cup (100 g) Pangrattato (page 26)

4 ounces (115 g) ground Parmigiano-Reggiano cheese, plus more to finish (see Work in Progress, page 66)

With a mortar and pestle, smash the garlic clove with a pinch of salt. Add the anchovies and smash into a uniform paste. The more smashed it all is, the better the dressing will be. Scrape every little bit into a small bowl and whisk in 4 teaspoons lemon juice, the Worcestershire sauce, and vinegar and season with salt and pepper. Twist a damp kitchen towel into a long snake and then lay it on the counter in a loop. Place a medium metal bowl inside the towel circle, which will keep the bowl from sliding around while whisking. Place the egg yolk and the remaining lemon juice into the metal bowl. Whisking constantly, very slowly drizzle a tiny bit of the olive oil at a time into the egg yolk. Go slowly to keep the emulsion from breaking. Once most of the oil is incorporated, you can let it go a bit faster; the mixture should be very thick. Now, whisk in the anchovy, lemon mixture, and ¾ of the ground Parmigiano-Reggiano cheese. Check the salt and acidity, adjusting the salt and lemon juice to taste. Check the texture of the dressing by dipping in a leaf—does it coat the leaf nicely but not too gloppily? If it needs thinning, add a teaspoon of water at a time to get the right texture.

(Recipe continues)

In a large bowl, toss the escarole leaves with the dressing—add a bit at a time to get the right amount of dressing for your taste. Taste and adjust the amount of salt and/or lemon juice if needed.

Place a nice layer of the dressed escarole on a large serving platter and sprinkle generously with the pangrattato. Build the salad up from there, mounding it up high and sprinkling the remaining pangrattato on top. Finish with a nice sprinkling of cheese and more black pepper, if you like.

Work in Progress: Not Always Delicate

Texture is a great tool in kitchen creativity. For this take on a Caesar, instead of croutons I use toasted breadcrumbs to create a more consistent crunch, and I tweak the cheese too. I love using my Microplane to make feathery shreds of cheese to top a bowl of silky pasta; in a crunch-fest like this salad, though, I actually prefer to grind my Parmigiano-Reggiano to a granular powder in the food processor. The rubbly texture matches the salad better than the fluffier gratings. And nobody would be upset if you just bought some nice Parmigiano-Reggiano ready-ground in a tub—that's what I do when I don't have time on my hands.

Melted Anchovy Toast

Serves 2 to 4

This preparation is all about the anchovy. Salty, garlicky, and spicy. It's messy, oily, and addictive.

This recipe actually was an accident. I had purchased some very fancy anchovies and was planning on just warming them to serve on toast, but they immediately liquified in the warm oil. And so I did what any rational person would do: I poured the resulting sauce onto a beautiful piece of toast and tasted it. So good, and among the easiest appetizers ever.

½ cup (120 ml) olive oil

10 anchovy fillets in oil

6 cloves garlic, thinly sliced

1 teaspoon red chile flakes

Zest of 1 lemon, cut into thin julienne slices

2 thick pieces sourdough bread, grilled or toasted well and cut into 4 pieces each

Basil leaves, to garnish

In a sauté pan, combine the olive oil, anchovy fillets, garlic, red chile flakes, and lemon zest. Slowly bring to a simmer over medium-low heat, stirring. Simmer for 2 to 3 minutes, until the garlic is soft and the anchovies have melted. I like to carefully turn the garlic slivers over so they cook evenly.

Place the toast on a platter and spoon the sauce evenly over the toast. Finish with basil leaves.

Work in Progress: No False Steps

Working creatively means being open to new paths as they arise. Here I was thinking I would just warm the anchovies to serve on toast, but they disintegrated into the oil and I was left with a wildly flavorful sauce to pour on the toast. Visually the anchovies slipped into the background and made a more mysterious and flavorful sauce to coat the toasted bread with. Being open to working with the unexpected—even the error—is the only way to relax and make the kitchen journey one of discovery rather than rule following. As Agnes Martin said about painting: "That which seems like the false step is just the next step."

Tomato Salad with Anchovy, Bayley Hazen Blue, and Big Croutons

Serves 4 to 6

There's a funny kind of amnesia that strikes each year when a highly seasonal ingredient reappears. Suddenly after not eating something for nine months or so, I am completely blown away by the succulence as if I'm tasting, say, fava beans, or new-crop walnuts, or, most obviously, garden-fresh tomatoes for the first time ever. How lucky we are to be able to feel that sense of wonder again, and for that reason, I pile on the tomato salads during tomato season, and fortunately, tomato salads are endlessly variable and reliably delicious. Then, just as sternly, I stop eating them altogether until the next summer comes along.

Since I also love a tomato sandwich, this salad effectively brings the sandwich to the salad, with giant hunks of crouton to soak up all the essential tomato flavors. The anchovies and blue cheese add funk and deepen the bright summer flavors.

6 large slices sourdough bread, ¾ inch (2 cm) thick

½ cup (120 ml) plus 3 tablespoons olive oil

¼ cup (60 ml) good red wine vinegar

1 teaspoon salt

Lots of freshly ground black pepper

2½ pounds (1.2 kg) beefsteak or heirloom tomatoes

8 anchovies, roughly chopped

Small bunch arugula, any variety (about 2 ounces/55 g)

5 ounces (140 g) Bayley Hazen blue cheese (or another buttery blue like Fourme d'Ambert), crumbled

Preheat the oven to 425°F (220°C).

Lay the bread out on a sheet pan and drizzle both sides with the 3 tablespoons olive oil. Toast for 10 minutes, then flip and toast for another 4 to 5 minutes, until the slices begin to brown but are still soft in the middle. Remove from the oven. When cool enough to handle, cut or tear the slices into irregular 2-inch (5 cm) chunks.

In a large bowl, whisk together the remaining ½ cup (120 ml) olive oil, the vinegar, salt, and pepper. Core the tomatoes and cut them into irregular chunks. Place the tomatoes and any extra juices in the bowl with the dressing and gently toss. Fold in the anchovies and toasted bread. Let sit for about 5 minutes.

Toss the tomatoes and bread again, and when you're ready to serve, gently fold in the arugula. Pile the salad onto a platter, spooning any liquid over the tomatoes and bread. Top with the crumbled cheese.

Burrata with Black Olive Tapenade and Tomato

Serves 4

Burrata, the creamier cousin of mozzarella, is always a favorite with guests because it is so luscious. That richness is best offset by a jolt of delicious saltiness, like from anchovies or olives, or in the case of this recipe, both ingredients at the same instant. Don't bother with the tomatoes if they aren't great. You could just use the olive mixture.

8 ounces (225 g) great-quality black olives, pitted (I like Taggiasca or oil-cured; see Note)

Pinch of red chile flakes

Grated zest of 1 lemon

Juice of ½ lemon, plus more as needed

1 small clove garlic, peeled

3 anchovies

¾ cup (45 g) soft green herbs, such as summer savory and/or basil, roughly chopped, plus leaves to finish

¼ cup (60 ml) olive oil, plus more to finish

Salt, as needed

6 beefsteak or heirloom tomatoes

1 large ball (4 to 6 ounces/115 to 170 g) burrata (burrata di bufala, if you can find it)

Flaky salt, to finish

Toasted bread, to serve

Put the olives, chile flakes, lemon zest and juice, garlic, anchovies, herbs, and olive oil in the bowl of a food processor fitted with a steel blade. Pulse quickly several times to get a rough-chopped texture. Check for seasoning and adjust with a bit of salt and/or lemon juice if desired.

Slice the tomatoes in irregular chunks and arrange them on a serving plate. Drizzle with a bit more olive oil and then add the tapenade in six or seven random piles all around the tomatoes. Place the burrata right on top! Top with some herb leaves and a bit of flaky salt. Finish with a few swishes of olive oil. Serve with the toasted bread.

Note: Buy olives with pits for better flavor and remove them yourself when needed. It's easiest to pit olives if you smoosh them first. I like to use the side of a chef's knife on a handful of olives at a time to get them to release their grip on their pits. Then I use my fingers to pull the pit away from the flesh.

Work in Progress: Celebrating Irregularity

There is a tradition in professional cooking of trying to cut irregular vegetables into perfectly regular shapes: perfectly turned potatoes, a tiny brunoise of carrots, and so forth. There can be reasons for such exacting standards, like even cooking times for each morsel, but I am often resistant to that regularity (and the waste that is generated by it). I try to find forms that reflect the organic shapes of each ingredient. I don't usually cut tomatoes into even slices or wedges. I like to respond to the wild variety of shapes that tomatoes take, whether bumpy heirloom giants or cherry tomatoes. I cut the tomatoes to reveal as much of their interesting structure as possible.

Braised Romano Beans with Anchovy, Chile Flakes, and Fancy Olive Oil

Serves 4 to 6

Broad Romano beans can be green, pale yellow, or a very flashy "dragon tongue," which is pale with streaks of purple—I love to grow that last variety in my backyard. I've never been a string bean lover, but Romano-style beans, which I discovered in my restaurant work and travels, are so full of luscious flavor. They are cooked with a very different mindset: not quickly blanched for crisp texture but slowly braised in a flavorful broth until they are silky and yielding. When I first visited Italy, long-cooked vegetables (with plenty of olive oil!) were new to me. You lose the bright color of a quick blanch, but in exchange, you get a velvety, rich flavor and texture, as perfectly satisfying as a meaty braise. A couple of prep notes: Make sure to pull the tough strings from your beans before cooking—they are even sturdier than those on string beans. And I like to leave the beans whole for twirly drama on the plate, but in truth they may be easier to eat with just a fork if you trim them into shorter sections. I will leave it up to you.

4 cloves garlic, thinly sliced

6 anchovy fillets, chopped

1 cup (240 ml) olive oil

2 pounds (910 g) Romano beans of any color, stemmed and strings removed, whole or cut into thirds

Peel of 1 lemon, thinly sliced

1½ teaspoons salt, plus more as needed

Large pinch of red chile flakes

10 basil leaves, plus more for garnish

Fancy olive oil, to drizzle

Flaky salt, to serve

In a large, heavy-bottomed pot over medium-low heat, warm the garlic and anchovies in the olive oil for about 2 minutes. Add ½ cup (120 ml) water, the beans, lemon peel, fine sea salt, and chile flakes and give them good stir. Cover and cook for about 1 hour, stirring every 5 to 10 minutes, until they are completely soft. Add the basil leaves and remove from heat. Let the basil infuse for at least 10 minutes, then serve. The beans can also be served at room temperature or refrigerated overnight. Don't serve them cold, though—rewarm them if you have refrigerated them. Garnish the beans with additional basil leaves (torn, if large), fancy olive oil, and flaky salt just before serving.

Late Summer Peppers with Melted Lemon, Anchovy, and Caper Butter and Pangrattato

Serves 4 to 6

Jimmy Nardello is a super-special, Italian-style sweet pepper that's just about as concentrated of a late summer delight as a ripe tomato or melon. They are wonderful to look at too: lipstick red and long, some curled tight like party noisemakers and others bending this way and that. To cook them, I usually just plonk them on a hot grill. They need very little else to make them special, so here I use two of my favorite old tricks: delicious toasted breadcrumbs and a big slice of compound butter, melted.

Neutral oil, to grease the grill

2 pounds (910 g) whole Jimmy Nardello or other sweet Italian roasting peppers (about 24)

¼ cup (60 ml) olive oil

Salt

4 ounces (115 g, about half a batch) Lemon, Anchovy, and Caper Compound Butter (page 62), melted

¾ cup (75 g) Pangrattato

Flaky salt, to finish

Prepare a charcoal grill. Once the coals are gray with bright red at their centers, spread them, but not too much: You want a very hot grill. Let the grate heat up for 5 minutes. While it is heating, brush it off and oil it using a pair of tongs and a paper towel drizzled with a bit of neutral oil.

In a large bowl, toss the peppers with the olive oil. Season lightly with salt.

Place the peppers on the grill in a single layer. Let them cook unbothered until richly browned on one side, about 4 minutes. Turn each pepper over and cook until the peppers are nicely browned and start to sag a bit when picked up (3 to 5 more minutes). Rearrange the peppers as they grill to make sure that the ones on the hotter spots of the grill don't get overcooked. As the peppers finish cooking, remove them to a cool plate.

To serve, arrange a layer of peppers on a serving platter or bowl. Generously spoon on some of the compound butter, then sprinkle with the breadcrumbs and a bit of flaky salt. Add another layer of peppers, then add the remaining compound butter and bread-crumbs and more flaky salt. Serve warm or at room temperature.

Runner beans in the garden

Green garlic scape butter

Pink platter with tomatoes

Mayocoba Beans on Toast with Anchovy, Sage, and Crème Fraîche

Serves 4 to 6

I didn't discover the starchy delight of beans on toast until I traveled through Umbria and Tuscany as a college student. The combination is so simple and rich and decadent and a wonderful textural combination, from the crunch of the grilled bread to the lovely mush of the beans. When I make my version, there are a few ways I push the texture and flavor. First, there's my favorite underpinning of anchovies, their umami flavor multiplied with a bit of Parmigiano broth. And then I make the beans extra luscious with lots of olive oil and a scoop of crème fraîche (I can never resist crème fraîche). Finally, I add an extra layer of crispness and earthiness by topping the beans with fried sage leaves.

8 ounces (225 g) dried Mayocoba beans, soaked overnight (try other beans, such as cannellini, flageolet, or even lima and cranberry)

1 tablespoon plus ½ teaspoon salt, plus more as needed

4 tablespoons (60 ml) olive oil

36 sage leaves

2 anchovy fillets, chopped

Pinch of red chile flakes

1 teaspoon red wine vinegar

1½ cups (360 ml) Parmigiano-Reggiano Broth (page 53)

½ cup (120 ml) crème fraîche

Freshly ground black pepper

Grated zest of 1 small lemon

¼ cup (25 g) pecorino Romano cheese

4 slices good sourdough bread

1 clove garlic, peeled

Fancy olive oil, to finish

Drain the beans. Place them in a large stockpot and add water to cover by at least 2 inches. Bring the beans to a boil and cook for 10 minutes. Lower the heat to maintain a simmer, add 1 tablespoon of the salt, and cook until beans are tender all the way through, 30 to 45 minutes (keep in mind bean cooking times can vary a lot—I find Mayocoba beans from Rancho Gordo or Yakima's Alvarez farm cook quite quickly). Drain the beans, let cool to lukewarm, and then refrigerate to cool completely.

Heat 2 tablespoons of the olive oil in a small heavy skillet over medium-high heat until a single sage leaf sizzles when placed in the oil. Have a plate lined with paper towels and a slotted spoon or spider ready. Place a handful of 8 to 10 leaves in the hot oil and stir to separate them. Cook, turning over once, for 10 to 15 seconds, until the leaves stiffen. Remove to the prepared plate and repeat with the remaining leaves, leaving about 12 smaller leaves uncooked.

(Recipe continues)

Pour the remaining 2 tablespoons olive oil into a large saucepan. Heat over medium-high heat and add the anchovies, uncooked sage leaves, and chile flakes. Cook for 30 seconds to 1 minute, until the anchovies dissolve into the oil a bit. Stir in the vinegar.

Add the drained beans and stir to coat. Pour in the Parmigiano-Reggiano broth and bring to a lively simmer. Stir in the remaining ½ teaspoon salt. Stay close to the pan and cook until the broth reduces by half, about 5 minutes.

Stir in the crème fraîche and reduce a bit more until the broth is creamy, about 3 minutes. Season generously with black pepper and stir in the lemon zest and cheese.

Toast the bread in a toaster (or in a pan if you prefer). As soon as each piece of bread emerges from the toaster, rub both sides with the garlic clove.

Place each piece of toast on a plate and spoon the beans and generous amounts of broth on and around the bread. Top each piece of toast with fried sage leaves, more black pepper, and a drizzle of fancy olive oil.

Work in Progress: Monochromatic Food

Some of the best tasting food in the world, including this dish, is kind of beigey-brown. It takes a little confidence to serve it without trying to brighten it up. Back in the nineties we would have felt the need to sprinkle a monochrome dish with parsley confetti. Here I garnish with a brownish-green fried sage leaf and just leave the earthy beauty of the rustic dish alone.

Chicken alla Cacciatore Sandwich with Rosemary, Vinegar, and Anchovies

Serves 4 to 6

Trapizzino is a chain that originated in Rome (and even has a NYC outpost) with an interesting concept: Stuff the classic saucy dishes of Rome into a chewy focaccia-like sandwich for luscious and portable feasting. I loved the food, especially a sandwich that boasted the super-tangy Roman take on chicken cacciatore inside, a chicken preparation that is all about the vinegar and herb intensity. Oh yes, and a fundamental anchovy savoriness. When I got home from that trip, I worked out my own take on the sandwich. My improvised version is still simple and stripped down but with a bit of aioli for extra luscious texture. Have extra napkins on hand for this one. A note on the bread: This is delicious no matter what, but you may want to try to find ciabatta rolls instead of a big loaf—the individual ciabattas are better at holding in all the juices. As it is, you'll want to eat quickly after assembling the sandwiches. You can do like my husband, Dan, and eat it while still standing up so the sandwich doesn't fall apart and you can dodge the drips if they start running down your arms.

4 skin-on chicken thighs, about 2¼ pounds (1.1 kg)

Salt

¼ cup (60 ml) olive oil

1½ cups (360 ml) red wine vinegar

1 cup (240 ml) white wine

2 (8-inch/20 cm) rosemary spears

5 cloves garlic, peeled

8 anchovies, chopped

Freshly ground black pepper

4 to 6 ciabatta rolls (or 1 large ciabatta loaf)

½ cup (120 ml) aioli (page 46)

Season the chicken thighs with salt. In a deep non-reactive skillet or saucepan, heat the olive oil over medium-high heat. Add the chicken pieces and fry until the skin is browned, 4 to 5 minutes. Turn the chicken pieces and brown on the other side, another 4 to 5 minutes.

Remove the chicken to a plate and reduce the heat to low. Remove the pan from the heat and add the vinegar, wine, and rosemary. Return the pan to the heat and scrape the pan to release the bits that have stuck. Add the garlic and anchovies and give it a stir. Then place the chicken back in the pan, making sure the skin is facing up. Put a lid on it and simmer over medium-low heat until very tender, 45 minutes to 1 hour.

(Recipe continues)

Remove the rosemary stems from the liquid and discard. Remove the chicken from the braising liquid, give the garlic cloves a smash, turn the heat up to medium-high, and reduce the liquid by half. Pluck the skin off the chicken and remove the bones from each thigh. Break the thighs into bite-sized chunks, then return the meat to the cooking liquid. Adjust the seasoning as needed with more salt and some pepper. The chicken can be made up to 2 days in advance and stored in an airtight container in the fridge. Re-warm the chicken on the stovetop until hot.

When you are ready to assemble the sandwiches, preheat the oven to 350°F (175°C).

You can flick water from a damp hand over the ciabatta rolls for extra crispiness. Place the rolls on a sheet pan and into the oven until crisp on the outside and warm throughout. Remove from the oven, and cut the rolls almost all the way through, like a pita. Slather the top of each roll with aioli and then generously scoop in the chicken chunks with their juices. Repeat with the remaining rolls and eat right away.

Roast Chicken with Anchovy, Ginger, and Crème Fraîche

Serves 4

I always try to be open to new flavors, even if sometimes for me a new flavor is an old flavor! In my home, ginger has recently gone from being an occasional aromatic to a kitchen essential. I think it's all the cooking I have done from the *Dishoom* cookbook from the glorious London collection of Indian restaurants. Sharp ginger mellows out beautifully in cooking, especially when partnered with other vivacious aromatics like cilantro or onions of all sorts. And it turns out ginger works beautifully in a crème fraîche marinade with umami-rich anchovies. Sour dairy like the yogurt in tandoori chicken or the crème fraîche in this recipe makes the best marinade—it tenderizes as it sits overnight and coaxes the chicken to a bubbly, perfectly blistered crackly skin. I like to serve this with a really sharp Dijon vinaigrette over butter lettuce or steamed fennel bulbs, and don't forget some bread for all the chicken fat you want to sop up.

Note: A trick I learned from *Dishoom* is how to save ginger before it gets all crinkly and old: Simply peel any leftover ginger root, chunk it up, and blend it to a puree with a little bit of water. Freeze the puree in ice cube trays and you've got ready-to-go ginger when you next need it!

1 cup (240 ml) crème fraîche

3-inch (7.5 cm) piece fresh ginger, peeled and grated

2 cloves garlic, roughly chopped

6 anchovy fillets

¼ bunch (13 g) Italian parsley (roughly chopped, stems are OK)

2 teaspoons salt

1 tablespoon olive oil

1 (3½- to 4-pound/1.6 to 1.8 kg) chicken, giblets removed

In a food processor or blender, blitz the crème fraîche, ginger, garlic, anchovies, parsley, salt, and olive oil until smooth. Rub the crème fraîche marinade all over and inside the whole chicken. Place uncovered on a plate in the fridge to dry out and marinate overnight. Pull the chicken from the refrigerator about 45 minutes before you plan to roast it.

Preheat the oven to 400°F (205°C) with a shelf ready in the middle of the oven.

Place the chicken on a roasting rack set on a roasting pan and roast for 20 minutes. Turn down the heat to 375°F (190°C) and roast until a thermometer inserted at the thickest part of the thigh measures 160°F (70°C), about 45 minutes. Remove from the oven, tent the chicken with foil, and let rest for 20 minutes. Carve and serve right away.

Roasted Bone-In Lamb Leg with Anchovy, Savory, and Fennel Seeds

Serves 8 to 10

Lamb and anchovies are one of the great flavor pairings—the funkiness of the lamb can meet and match the potent umami of a paste-like anchovy marinade. Cooked low and slow, it's a perfect laid-back dinner party showpiece. (I have a bay laurel tree in my backyard, so I like to serve the meat on a fragrant bed of its branches—not essential but so pretty.)

6 anchovies, minced

3-inch (7.5 cm) piece fresh ginger, peeled and grated

4 cloves garlic, grated

1 teaspoon fennel seeds, toasted and crushed

1 tablespoon savory leaves, chopped

2 tablespoons sweet paprika

4 teaspoons salt

½ cup (120 ml) olive oil

1 (6- to 7-pound/2.7 to 3.2 kg) trussed bone-in leg of lamb

2 or 3 bay laurel branches, if available

1 batch Ginger Green Sauce (page 25)

In a small bowl, mix the anchovies, ginger, garlic, fennel seeds, savory, paprika, salt, and olive oil. Rub the resulting paste all over the leg of lamb. Place the lamb on a plate and refrigerate uncovered for at least 4 hours or overnight.

When you are ready to cook the lamb, preheat the oven to 325°F (165°C).

Roast the lamb until an instant-read thermometer inserted at the thickest part of the leg reads 135°F (57°C), 1½ to 2 hours. It will have a nice medium cook (what I generally prefer on legs of lamb). Let the leg rest for at least 15 minutes before carving. Parade around the dinner table with your lovely roast before slicing it—I like to cut down to the bone and remove big hunks, which I then thinly slice, working as best as I can to slice across the grain of each piece.

Arrange the bay laurel and sliced lamb on a warm platter and serve a bowl of ginger green sauce on the side.

___

Work in Progress: Reconsidering Old Tools

In the same way an artist may revisit a medium they put aside—maybe Conté crayons or oil sticks— a cook sometimes needs to rethink ingredients they have sidelined (like I have done with ginger). Work with them again after a few years and see if they might seem fresh again. Try them in a different context or in different proportions than you might have in the past. Balsamic vinegar and dried tomatoes (page 29) both got overplayed in restaurants for a while, but recently they have come back joyfully into my pantry.

Unfussy Old Favorites

Lifelong Lessons

One of the questions for the ages, in food, in visual art, and in writing, too, is: "When is it done?" When does something have enough going for it to be presented to the public? There is no one set answer—an omelet with no filling can be perfect, as can a filigreed, multi-textured Parisian gâteau. But still, "Is it finished?" is a crucial question for the creative person to ask. It attempts to determine if a creative work is approaching the intention of the artist. As I get older, more and more often I find that the food I make needs fewer elements to feel finished.

In truth, I have always leaned toward simplicity in food. Early on, I thought it was because it was easier: I didn't have formal cooking training before I found myself running a restaurant. Now I know that's not always the case—simplicity leaves you and your technique exposed. There's a confident elegance to plain food, and I like that.

I've been thinking about where my inclination to simplify came from. When I was growing up in the seventies and eighties, there were a lot of ingredients that were not easily available to us in the Northwest— ingredients that I can't imagine living without today: really good olive oil, really good olives for that matter, the full range of greens from Belgian endive to darkest lacinato kale, or any number of delicious chiles from Korea, Mexico, or Vietnam. But the stuff we did have regularly was so good—my parents fed us well, drawing directly from the earth and the sea as much as they could.

We regularly gobbled up fresh-caught coho and pink salmon, crab, clams, and shrimp. The summer garden was full of tomatoes and carrots and beans, and in the winter, Mom had preserved so many of them in jars that we kept in pretty rows under the stairs. Looking back, I realize how much I picked up from their example. So, when I put together recipes that have a retro flair to them—mayonnaise-basted salmon or a chunky meat loaf sandwich—I am touching back to those early lessons in simple, quality, seasonal food. This chapter is filled with lots of uncomplicated seafood and summer vegetables: ingredients I grew up eating or learned to cook in my earliest restaurant days.

Restraint was a virtue for me when I found myself owning an often-understaffed restaurant at twenty-five years old. I took my lessons in French casualness from Boat Street's founder, Susan Kaplan, but to her original menu I added stripped-down items like steamed salmon with hollandaise and chives, lettuces with Dijon vinaigrette and roasted walnuts, pound cake with soft whipped cream and berries. The roasted pork loin sandwich (page 98) in this chapter was a Boat Street staple. It is monochromatically beige, but beautifully so, and its flavor is unforgettable. At the time I first started serving it and similar dishes, I thought I was making things simpler just so I could get them out of the kitchen and onto my guests' tables. But now, with more skill and more staff, I love these things more than ever.

Travel has also shown me a certain kind of traditional minimalism I cannot resist. I have eaten the most elaborate meals you can imagine: plates dusted with powders, dotted with elegant sauces, puffed foams still smoking from the liquid nitrogen that froze them. All of this is engaging—often delicious. But when I travel, the food I keep coming back to is the simplest stuff, rooted deep in traditions: in London, a piece of white fish with mousseline sauce and the most perfect Jersey Royal potatoes, say, or a Roman salad of chicories dressed with just olive oil, garlic, and anchovies. These foods are simple, yes, but they are also clear and confident. They linger in my memory long after the meal.

Now, as a mentor to other cooks in my restaurants, I find that one of the hardest things is teaching people when to stop adding. We all are constantly learning about new ingredients, and the desire to use them is real: It's possible to get ingredient FOMO. But it's our job to edit and know when something is too much. There are many reasons that we teach restraint: It can more directly honor culinary traditions; reduce waste; or present bolder, clearer flavors. There is still room for creativity in this restrained approach. A dish must always find that special hook: maybe a novel presentation, a delightful textural component, or a disarming condiment. But everything must be in balance—a cook has so many meals to prepare in a lifetime, not everything has to appear on a single plate. As I look back, I can see that I have always sought the calm and clarity of simplicity in my cooking. These days, I am just able to claim it more proudly, and I hope I can give other cooks, including you, the confidence to proudly serve elegantly restrained food.

Tuna Melt with Charred Jalapeño Pickles, Chives, and Provolone

Serves 4

Sometimes you barely want to cook but you are still hungry for something delicious. That's when a tuna melt can come to the rescue. One day a couple of years ago, Seattle was saddled with a "heat dome" and the temperatures rose well about 100°F (38°C), blasting through previous record highs. My friends were hanging out at their houseboat. We needed a little dinner, but I couldn't bear the idea of much cooking. So, I put together a few tuna melts—it took about ten minutes—and we ate them with our feet dangling in the lake and a pile of cold cherries to accompany them. Inspired by that hot day, I made an extra-snappy version of the classic toasted sandwich: spicy charred jalapeño pickles and peppery provolone lend extra punch. The melts would be extra-delicious to eat on a hot summer day with your feet dangling in the lake (or just a kiddie pool).

4 hearty slices sourdough bread

2 charred and pickled jalapeños (see page 33), seeds removed, diced (about 2 ounces/60 g)

½ cup (10 g) chopped chives

2 heaping tablespoons salted capers, soaked in fresh water for at least 15 minutes, drained, and chopped

½ white onion (about 6 ounces/ 160 g), minced

1 fresh serrano chile, minced

½ cup (120 ml) mayonnaise

1 (9-ounce/250 g) can good-quality tuna in oil (I use St. Jude's, but also love Arroyabe and Ortiz)

7 ounces (200 g) provolone cheese, shredded (ideally a sharp Italian brand)

Place an oven rack in the center of the oven and turn on the broiler.

Lightly toast the bread and set it aside.

In a medium bowl, mix the jalapeño chiles, chives, capers, onion, serrano chile, mayonnaise, and tuna. Divide the tuna evenly among the toast slices. Cover each with shredded cheese and place on a sheet pan. Place under the broiler. Keep a close eye on the toasts as they broil: The goal is tuna that has warmed up and cheese that is super melty and browned; broilers vary greatly, but about 4 minutes.

Serve warm, and don't forget to eat all the crispy cheese from the pan too.

My Favorite Spaghetti with Clams, Crème Fraîche, and Green Herbs

Serves 4

At the University of Washington, I lived in a crumbling apartment that made my parents worry. But I felt like a real adult for the first time and was proud to cook for myself in my hand-me-down Farberware pots. Like a lot of students, I made a lot of pasta, including a take on my mom's spaghetti with clam sauce. These days I have a prettier kitchen and heavier pots, but I still like to make spaghetti with clams. Except now I tweak it with tarragon and crème fraîche.

3 pounds (1.4 kg) manila clams

½ cup (120 ml) olive oil

1 bottle (750 ml) dry white wine

4 cloves garlic, sliced

Salt

1 pound (455 g) spaghetti

1 tablespoon unsalted butter

Zest of 1 lemon, julienned (about ⅔ ounce/18 g)

½ cup (120 ml) crème fraîche

2 cups (120 g) Italian parsley leaves

2 cups (120 g) tarragon leaves

Freshly ground black pepper

Lemon juice, if needed

3 tablespoons fancy olive oil, for finishing

Calabrian chili oil (or your favorite hot condiment), to serve

Lemon wedges, to serve

Flaky salt, to serve

Prep the clams by rinsing them very well in multiple changes of water until there is no sand left in the water.

In a large saucepan, warm the olive oil, wine, and garlic over medium-low heat. Bring to a gentle simmer and simmer for 5 minutes. Turn the heat up to medium and add the clams. Cover the pot and steam for 1 minute, then take the lid off and remove the clams one by one as they open.

When all the clams are cooked, strain the liquid through a fine sieve and reserve it.

To finish, bring a large pot of water to a boil. Generously salt the water. Add the spaghetti, stir well, and cook according to the package instructions, 5 to 8 minutes, until al dente. Stir often so the pasta does not stick to the bottom of the pot.

While the pasta is cooking, place a large sauté pan over medium heat. Add 1½ cups (360 ml) of the clam liquid, the butter, and lemon peel. With a spider or tongs, remove the spaghetti from the water and place in the pan with the clam liquid and ¼ cup (60 ml) water. Toss well, bring to a boil, and cook for about a minute to let the liquid absorb.

Turn the heat down to low and toss in the clams, crème fraîche, parsley, and tarragon. Thin out with more clam juice if needed. Taste and adjust the seasoning with additional salt, black pepper, and/or a spritz of lemon juice. Drizzle with the fancy olive oil and serve with Calabrian chili oil, a wedge of lemon, and flaky salt on the side.

Just a Pork Loin Sandwich

Serves 10 to 12

Here's a confession: I like boring sandwiches. Maybe boring is an extreme way to put it, but I like sandwiches that are direct and simple, not necessarily piled high and spread with four different condiments. Case in point, the great roast beef sandwiches with onion and mayo on sliced Poulsbo sunflower bread that my mom made me in my childhood. I also love salami and butter sandwiches as well as pâté and cornichon baguettes. Sandwiches like these aren't dull; they are just minimal enough that you can focus on the main ingredients. And so, this pork loin sandwich, a favorite at Boat Street Café, is in the same model. It's perfect for serving a crowd or for taking on an outing for outdoor noshing. When choosing your loin, ask your butcher for the shoulder end, if possible, as the other end is leaner, and you are looking for an even layer of fat here.

Note: I obviously love raw onions, with their crisp, slightly hot crunch. If you are on the fence about them, try this trick—soak the sliced onions in cold water for a few minutes to remove some of the liquid that comes off the onion and soften the flavor. Pat them dry with a paper towel before using.

1 teaspoon salt, plus more for the sandwiches

2 teaspoons freshly ground black pepper, plus more for the sandwiches

¾ cup (180 ml) Dijon mustard (I like Fallot brand)

½ cup (70 g) rosemary needles, minced (from about 4 sprigs)

2 cloves garlic, grated

4 pounds (1.8 kg) boneless pork loin (not tenderloin)

3 baguettes or other crusty bread

1 white onion, thinly sliced (about ¼ inch/6 mm thick; see Note)

Mayonnaise, to serve

The day before serving, make a mixture of the salt, pepper, mustard, rosemary, and garlic. Rub all over the pork loin and refrigerate overnight. Remove from the fridge 45 minutes before cooking.

Preheat the oven to 425°F (220°C).

Put the marinated pork loin directly on a roasting pan, fat side up. Roast for 20 minutes, then reduce the oven temperature to 225°F (110°C) and continue to roast until the center of the loin measures 135°F (57°C) on a quick-read thermometer. Remove from the oven, tent with aluminum foil, and let cool to room temperature. The loin can be served immediately or refrigerated to serve cold the next day.

Slice the pork loin very thinly. Cut the baguettes lengthwise, leaving one side attached to make a hinge. Coat the cut sides generously with mayonnaise. Shingle the pork in overlapping slices inside the bread. Lay onion slices across the pork. Season with salt and pepper. Cut baguettes crosswise into sandwiches.

98

West Coast Crab Cakes
(by this I mean Dungeness crab cakes)

Serves 6

I'll take a moment here to say I understand this is an expensive recipe. Or it's expensive if you can't catch your own crab! You have to understand that in the Pacific Northwest, "crab" is as much a verb as a noun. On a recent trip, I joined my friends Bernie and Christy in the Salish Sea outside Edison, Washington, and were we ever lucky. A couple of hours after tossing our baited crab pots, we hauled in fifteen lunkers (see photo on page 100). It was the biggest catch of the past few years. Naturally, we ate some steamed with drawn butter that evening, but the next day, we got to work with the remaining crabmeat and made these chunky and delicious crab cakes. No matter if you catch your own or decide to splurge on some crabmeat, crab cakes are always a cause for celebration.

(Recipe continues)

For the corn salad:

1 small red onion, thinly sliced

2 ears corn, kernels cut off the cob

1 pint (290 g) cherry tomatoes, sliced in half

½ cup (120 ml) olive oil

Grated zest of 1 lime

Juice of 2 limes (about ¼ cup/60 ml) juice, plus more as needed

1 teaspoon salt, plus more as needed

Lots of freshly ground black pepper

½ ounce (14 g) cilantro leaves (basically a big handful of cilantro leaves and a bit of stem too)

For the crab cakes:

3 large eggs

1 cup (240 ml) heavy cream

1 teaspoon Dijon mustard

1 tablespoon brown sugar

1½ teaspoons salt

½ teaspoon red chile flakes

2½ pounds (1.2 kg) cooked Dungeness crab meat, from about 4 crabs

1 small yellow onion, finely minced

¼ cup (15 g) thyme leaves

½ cup (30 g) Plain Dried Breadcrumbs (page 26)

3 serrano chiles, minced (seeds removed if you want it less spicy)

6 tablespoons (85 g) clarified butter or purchased ghee (see Note)

2 cups (240 g) coarse-ground cornmeal (I like Bob's Red Mill)

First, assemble the corn salad: In a small bowl, soak the red onion slices in cold water for 15 minutes. Drain them and firmly pat dry with paper towels. Mix the onions, corn, cherry tomatoes, olive oil, lime zest and juice, salt, and black pepper to taste in a small bowl. Let sit for 10 minutes, or cover and store in the fridge until serving time. It's great both cold and at room temperature.

Next, make the crab cakes: In a medium bowl, whisk together the eggs, cream, mustard, brown sugar, ½ teaspoon of the salt, and the chile flakes. In a large bowl, combine the crab, onion, thyme, breadcrumbs, and chiles and mix well. Fold in the egg mixture to distribute evenly throughout the crab mixture. Portion the crab cakes into roughly 6 cakes about 1¼ inches (3 cm) thick.

Preheat the oven to 400°F (205°C).

Heat a 10- to 12-inch (25 to 30 cm) heavy skillet over medium-high heat. When hot, add 2 tablespoons of the clarified butter. As it bubbles, sprinkle one side of 3 crab cakes with a generous coating of cornmeal. Place the crab cakes cornmeal side down in the pan, then add 1 more tablespoon of the clarified butter. Cook for about 3 minutes, until deeply golden brown. Remove the 3 crab cakes to a plate, pour out any remaining cornmeal and butter from the pan, and wipe clean. Repeat the frying process with the remaining 3 crab cakes. When all are cooked on one side, sprinkle the naked side of each crab cake with cornmeal. Flip the ones still in the skillet gently and add back the 3 from the first batch, uncooked, cornmeal-sprinkled side down. Place the pan in the oven. Bake for 5 minutes, or until crispy on the bottom.

When you are ready to eat, gently fold the cilantro into the corn salad. Check for seasoning and adjust with salt, pepper, and/or lime juice as needed. Serve the warm crab cakes nestled beside the corn salad, letting a bit of the salad sit on top of each cake.

Note: You can get well-priced ghee at Trader Joe's and Indian specialty grocers. There's less chance of burning the crab cakes when you use clarified butter or ghee rather than regular butter.

Gorgeous summer night on Vashon

Dungeness crabs & ferns

Spee-bi-dah Sea Smoke

Slow-Cooked Zucchini with Basil, Garlic, and Olive Oil

Serves 6 to 8

Here's an Italian-inspired stewy vegetable dish of the kind I love so much. With enough good olive oil and garlic, firm, small-gauged zucchini becomes a perfect no-effort stew to eat on a hot summer night with ripped-off hunks of bread and a bit of sharp ricotta salata or pecorino. This method of cooking also works well for onions, peppers, beans (see page 81), and more. Ingredients cooked this way are wonderful both at room temperature and chilled (though you don't want them too cold, or the olive oil will still be solid—take them out of the fridge fifteen minutes before serving, and make sure to add a big glug of spicy olive oil before you serve.

½ cup (120 ml) olive oil

2 cloves garlic, peeled

3½ pounds (1.6 kg) small zucchini, sliced into ½-inch (12 mm) coins

1 teaspoon salt, plus more as needed

2½ cups (100 g) whole basil leaves

Flaky salt and freshly ground black pepper, to serve

Fancy olive oil, to garnish

Toast (optional)

Freshly shaved ricotta salata or pecorino cheese (optional)

In a large pot with a lid, heat the olive oil with the garlic over medium-low heat for 1 minute. Add the zucchini and give it a big stir. Stir in the fine sea salt. Cover and reduce the heat to medium-low. Cook for 40 minutes, stirring every 5 minutes so the zucchini does not stick to the bottom and brown. After 40 minutes, the zucchini will become very soft, almost like zucchini jam. Remove the lid and let the water steam out for 8 to 10 minutes.

Remove the pot from heat and stir in the basil leaves. They will darken and release their amazing flavor. Check for seasoning, adding salt if necessary and a bunch of pepper. Serve right away warm or, later, cold, always with a drizzle of fancy olive oil and a sprinkle of flaky salt. Try it on toast topped with ricotta salata or pecorino.

Sweet Corn Flan with Spinach, Beecher's Cheddar, and Marjoram

Serves 8

This was a dish Susan taught me at Boat Street. If the name is a bit intimidating, just think of it as a puffy casserole. Originally it was served in a low bowl, making it easier and faster to cook. But craving a bit of color and drama, we gradually migrated it to a large soufflé dish, where we piled it high with spinach, other select vegetables, cheese, and custard. It took forty minutes to fire each order, driving us all crazy, as it threw off the pace of the line every time. But the flan was so pretty and so delicious, it was hard to let go. Since I closed Boat Street, it hasn't appeared on other menus because of the long cooking time, but I keep hearing fond memories of it from guests and friends. At home it is less likely to mess up your timing, making it the perfect dish for a celebration. This is even bigger than the original, so you can enjoy it with a group of friends or family. I love it on its own as a hearty veggie main course with a spicy Dijon dressed salad, and it also makes a delicious side to a perfectly roasted chicken.

Note: You could substitute Oven-Dried Tomatoes (page 29) for the corn or use both.

(Recipe continues)

4 large eggs

4 cups (960 ml) heavy cream

¼ teaspoon cayenne pepper

Several gratings fresh nutmeg (about ¼ teaspoon)

1 teaspoon salt, plus more as needed

1 cup (90 g) grated Parmigiano-Reggiano cheese

20 ounces (570 g) spinach (that's 2 giant containers of cleaned baby spinach)

4 ears corn, kernels cut off the cob

Freshly ground black pepper

1 large (30 g) Fresno chile, thinly sliced

1 cup (60 g) picked marjoram leaves

8 ounces (225 g) grated Beecher's Flagship sharp white cheddar cheese or other cheddar

Flaky salt, to finish

Place an oven rack in a center slot and remove any racks above it: This flan puffs up like a soufflé. Preheat the oven to 400°F (205°C).

In a large bowl, whisk the eggs with the cream, then whisk in the cayenne, nutmeg, salt, and Parmigiano-Reggiano cheese.

Place a deep 9½ × 13-inch (24 cm × 33 cm) gratin dish on a sheet pan and pile two-thirds of the spinach inside it. It will look like a ridiculous amount, yet as it cooks, it will all compress down, so trust me you will need it all. Carefully place half of the corn kernels on top of the spinach and let them fall into all the gaps between leaves. Scatter with salt and black pepper, then add the remaining spinach and corn and the chile and season with salt and pepper again. Gradually pour the egg mixture over the corn and spinach one ladleful at a time, making sure it settles before adding more. You can pull the spinach toward the center of the dish and add the liquid at the perimeter to keep the liquid from spilling off the leaves. When about three-quarters of the egg mixture is in the dish, evenly scatter in the marjoram and the cheddar cheese. Finish by ladling in the remaining egg mixture and lightly sprinkling with flaky salt.

Place it in the middle of the oven and bake until browned, puffed, and no longer wobbly at the center, about 1 hour and 20 minutes, covering the flan lightly with foil for the last 30 minutes or so to keep the top from burning. Serve right away (it will deflate).

Frisée Salad with Croutons, Poached Eggs, and Bacon

Serves 4

This is a dreamy dinner salad and, of course, a Parisian bistro classic, with a forceful mustard dressing, bacon fat–fried croutons, and a soft poached egg with a yolk that functions as a second dressing for the salad. Do take time to get the details right here—slow-toasting the croutons in the bacon fat and trimming the frisée carefully. Make sure to serve the salad right away so the egg is seductively warm (you can take some pressure off by poaching the eggs earlier in the day and then re-warming them in simmering water just before serving).

For the Dijon vinaigrette:

1 clove garlic, finely grated

3 tablespoons Dijon mustard

Salt and freshly ground black pepper

3 tablespoons excellent-quality white wine vinegar or champagne vinegar

6 tablespoons (90 ml) olive oil

For the salad:

8 to 10 ounces (225 to 280 g) thick-cut bacon, cut on a bias into about ¾-inch (2 cm) pieces

2 heads frisée, when trimmed about 12 ounces (340 g), green parts cut off

1 teaspoon white wine vinegar

6 cups torn crustless bread (about 1 pound/455 g)

4 large eggs

Fancy olive oil

Flaky salt and freshly ground black pepper

A handful of matchstick-cut chives

Make the vinaigrette: In a small bowl, whisk together the garlic, mustard, and salt and pepper to taste, then whisk in the vinegar. Slowly drizzle in the olive oil while whisking. Set aside. This is a super-easy and stable dressing.

Make the salad: Fry the bacon in a large skillet over medium heat until it is crispy. Scoop the bacon out of the fat (reserve the fat!) and lay the bacon pieces on a plate lined with paper towels.

While the bacon is cooking, put the frisée in a large bowl.

Bring a medium pot of water to boil. Add the vinegar and turn the heat down to a very lazy simmer.

Return the skillet with the bacon fat in it to the stove-top and heat over medium heat. Add the bread and toast the croutons, taking care to turn the croutons individually and brown them deeply on all sides. If you run low on fat, you can add a bit of olive oil to the pan to aid the browning.

When the croutons are halfway done, gently slide the eggs to be poached into the boiling water. Try to keep the water at a gentle simmer, not a rolling boil, or you will separate the whites of your eggs. They will take 2 to 3 minutes to poach (for a very soft set egg), and it is easiest to do two at a time rather than all four. Using a slotted spoon or a spider, lift

(Recipe continues)

the eggs from the water when they are done and dab them gently with a paper towel to remove any excess water. You can poach the eggs in advance and remove them to an ice-water bath when finished. Before serving, put them in a bath of simmering water to warm through; this takes less than 1 minute.

Once the croutons are browned on all sides and crispy, lift them out of the bacon fat and put them in the bowl with the frisée. While the croutons are warm, pour over the Dijon vinaigrette, sprinkle in most of the chives, and toss everything well. Double-check the salt and pepper and adjust as desired. Divide the salad evenly among 4 plates.

Place a poached egg on each salad. Drizzle fancy olive oil over the egg and finish with a pinch of flaky salt, more freshly ground pepper, and chives. Eat right away so the egg yolk will run into the salad.

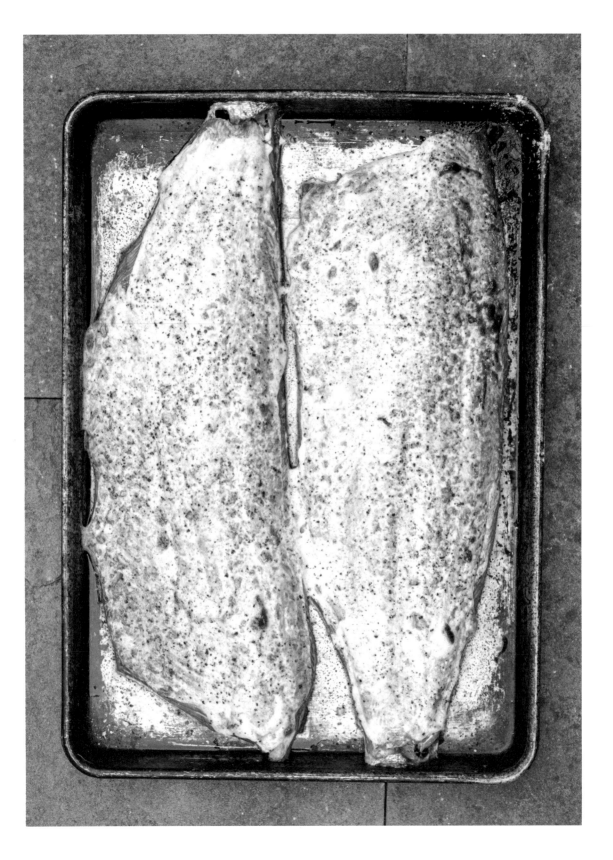

1970s Mom's Mayo-Slathered Salmon

Serves 8 or more as part of a picnic

Those who know me well know my love for mayonnaise. Of course, I love homemade aioli and other types of mayonnaise, but I also find that commercial mayonnaise, specifically Best Foods, is an MVP in the kitchen. I lavish it into tomato sandwiches, buzz it into green goddess dressing, and here in a throwback move, deploy it as a marinade. The fat in the mayo keeps the salmon moist, and the protein encourages the surface to get all bubbly and brown. My mom mostly grilled salmon on a piece of foil, and you can, too, if you have the setup, but it is also wonderful cooked in a hot oven. When I have time I like serving it with a big herb salad built on a base of Little Gem lettuce, piled up with tons of mint, cilantro, and dill, and drizzled with some olive oil, lemon juice, and salt.

⅓ cup (75 ml) mayonnaise

1 teaspoon lemon juice

4 pounds (1.8 kg) wild sockeye salmon (about 2 filleted sides), scaled, trimmed, and pin bones removed (see Note, page 122)

1 teaspoon salt

Lots of freshly ground black pepper

Preheat the oven to 400°F (205°C). Line a sturdy sheet pan with parchment paper.

In a small bowl, mix the mayonnaise and lemon juice. Place the fillets on the prepared sheet pan and evenly slather the top side with the mayonnaise mixture. Season with the salt and a generous grinding of black pepper. Place the pan in the oven and cook for about 12 minutes. You want the thickest part just barely firm to the touch. I like a bit of translucence at the center of the fillet if possible. Pull the salmon from the oven and let it rest for about 5 minutes before serving on a pretty platter.

Work in Progress: Making Use of Castoffs

Artists are great scavengers of odds and ends to incorporate into their work, and I am, too, when it comes to little bits of leftovers from last night's dinner. Extra salmon's a particularly useful thing to cook with the next day. For instance, you could make a wonderful salmon fried rice topped with any herbs you have on hand and dollops of chili crisp. Or keep things simple and flake it up with more mayonnaise (of course!) and a bit of finely chopped red onion or chives. I'd serve it on a thick slice of sourdough toast and crown it with some lightly dressed arugula from my garden.

Misty summer morning

The beach at Spee-bi-dah

Fishing village on Puget Island

Pan-Roasted Sockeye Salmon with Hazelnut and Parsley Sauce

Serves 4 to 6

Salmon choices matter. If we manage things correctly, gorgeous Bristol Bay sockeye will be around for a lot longer. I wish we could say that for so many of the other salmon runs in the Northwest. Salmon is in trouble, and farmed salmon is gross (flabby in taste, and it pollutes the ocean). If you run into me sometime, I will let you know all the ways that farming is the wrong way to bring more salmon to the market. I will also encourage you to consider eating frozen fish, which allows you to be picky about the salmon you eat because you can order directly from well-managed fisheries—like the fish from Eva's Wild, which can be shipped around the country to you! Frozen at sea, the quality of good frozen fish is often better than the "fresh" (usually thawed anyway) at the local market.

6 ounces (170 g) hazelnuts (Washington-grown Holmquist hazelnuts come dry-roasted and are fantastic)

½ cup (65 g) minced shallot

1 cup (60 g) Italian parsley leaves

2 tablespoons red wine vinegar

1 cup (240 ml) hazelnut oil

2 teaspoons Dijon mustard

2 teaspoons salt, plus more as needed

Grated zest of 1 lemon

1 tablespoon lemon juice, plus more as needed

2 pounds (910 g) center-cut sockeye salmon fillet, skin on (see Note on pinbones below)

3 tablespoons olive oil

Preheat the oven to 350°F (175°C).

Place the hazelnuts on a rimmed sheet pan and toast, tossing occasionally, until pale golden brown at their centers, 6 to 8 minutes. Let cool. Place in a mortar and pestle and crush them: Big pieces are OK, but make sure there aren't any whole nuts. (This should be chunkier than if done in a food processor.) If you don't have a mortar and pestle, you can put the nuts in a bag and smash them with a rolling pin or wooden mallet.

Soak the shallots in cold water for 5 minutes. Drain well, pressing with a folded paper towel to blot up the moisture. In a medium bowl, mix the crushed hazelnuts, parsley, shallot, vinegar, hazelnut oil, mustard, 1 teaspoon of the salt, the lemon zest, and lemon juice. Stir well and adjust the seasoning with more salt and lemon juice if desired. This can be stored in the refrigerator for a few hours or even overnight. Make sure there is enough oil to cover the chunks.

With a sharp knife, lightly score the skin side of the salmon fillet—about 6 crisscross incisions on the fatter side of the fillet. Season the fish with the remaining 1 teaspoon salt.

(Recipe continues)

In a large (12-inch/30 cm) skillet, heat the olive oil over high heat until it shimmers. Place the fish in the pan flesh side down and shake the pan a bit to keep the fillets from adhering to the pan. Turn the heat down to medium and cook until the fish turns opaque about two-thirds of the way up the cut ends, about 3 minutes. Be careful, as the oil may pop and spit. Using a large fish spatula, carefully turn over the fillets. Turn the heat back up to high and shake again for about 30 seconds. Baste the skin with the accumulated juices. Turn the heat down, cover with a lid, and cook for 2 more minutes. Poke at the highest part of the fillet. If it flakes, it is done. If not, cover and cook for a bit longer. When done, remove the fillet to a plate.

Taste the hazelnut sauce and adjust with more salt or lemon juice if desired. With your hands, break the salmon into chunks and place it on serving plates. Stir the hazelnut sauce and spoon it generously on each portion. Serve with additional sauce on the side.

Note: Feel along the ridge of the fillet about two-thirds of the way from the tail; you'll feel a gentle poke from a line of flexible bones called pinbones; you can pull them out with a pair of (clean) tweezers. Find a bone with your finger, pinch it with your tweezers, and pull toward the wide end of the fish. Repeat until you've got them all!

Work in Progress: Tap into Memories

I understand that not everyone feels nostalgic for salmon. If you grew up landlocked, it's likely that the seaborn fish you ate wasn't as signally fresh and pink and plump as the ones my dad and our neighbors caught midsummer. The seas have changed since I was a kid, and I don't serve the most endangered species of salmon in my restaurants, but I still adore cooking and eating coho, sockeye, and pink salmon— it takes me back to the wonderful wilder moments of my childhood (that's why I provide two salmon recipes in this chapter). For you, nostalgia might taste different: peach pie, fried chicken, or a hearty stew. But don't give up on chasing those flavors of your youth: They offer powerful motivation in the kitchen.

Poached Halibut with Sorrel Sauce

Serves 2 to 4, with 1½ cups (360 ml) sorrel sauce

Poaching fish isn't as popular as when I first started cooking at Boat Street. I think that people like the flash of the grill and crunchy skin coaxed out of a hot skillet. Poaching is such a lovely technique, though, and perfect for a lean fish like halibut, which tends to dry out during cooking. It's time to bring the method back! Poaching is best done with a flavorful liquid, called a court bouillon in French, which lends extra flavor to the gentle cooking method. Halibut emerges snow white and so tender from the pot. For a tangy sauce, another old-fashioned flavor: sorrel, the lemony herb that is as easy to grow in the garden as it is hard to find in a grocery store. If you don't have any at your local market, you could substitute watercress. This dish is beautiful with another ivory and green creation, Mom's Potato Salad (page 162).

For the sorrel sauce:

2 ounces (55 g) sorrel leaves, roughly chopped

⅓ cup (75 ml) heavy cream

¾ cup (180 ml) sour cream

2 tablespoons olive oil (maybe more), plus more to serve

1 clove garlic

1 teaspoon salt

1 teaspoon freshly ground black pepper

Lemon juice, if needed

(Ingredients continue)

First, make the sorrel sauce: Using a high-powered blender, buzz the sorrel, heavy cream, sour cream, 2 tablespoons of the olive oil, the garlic, salt, and pepper. Process until smooth and pale, bright green, then taste and adjust with more salt and/or some lemon juice, if desired. Set aside. The sauce can be made up to 1 day ahead and kept in an airtight container in the refrigerator.

Poach the fish: Tie the parsley and thyme together with a bit of kitchen twine. Place it in a large (3- to 4-quart/2.8 to 3.8 liter) nonreactive stockpot. Add 4 cups (960 ml) water, the peppercorns, fennel, garlic, wine, lemon zest, salt, and 2 tablespoons olive oil. Slowly bring the poaching ingredients to a boil over medium heat and then turn down the heat to maintain a simmer. Cook for 10 minutes. Gently slide in the fillet of halibut and cook at a bare simmer until the fish is opaque all the way to the center, 10 to 12 minutes (this can vary with the thickness of the fillet—it's OK to poke a knife into an unobtrusive spot and check doneness).

(Recipe continues)

For the fish and assembly:

6 stems parsley

4 sprigs thyme

10 black peppercorns

½ fennel bulb, cut into 4 wedges

2 cloves garlic, smashed and peeled

1 cup (240 ml) white wine

Zest of ½ lemon (use a peeler to make a ribbon of zest)

½ teaspoon salt, plus more to finish

2 tablespoons olive oil

1 pound (450 g) filleted halibut, center cut, if possible, one whole piece

Spicy olive oil, to finish

Mixed tender green herb leaves, to garnish (a combination of parsley, basil, tarragon, chervil, and/or chives)

Tiny radishes, to serve (optional)

Remove the fish from the poaching liquid with a slotted spatula and place on a clean cloth to remove any excess water. Place the halibut on the serving plate. Season with a touch of sea salt, generously spoon the sorrel sauce over the fish, drizzle with some spicy olive oil, and finish with lots of green herbs. And if it is spring and you can find them, garnish with some dainty radishes with their greens.

Work in Progress: Cooking for Your Mood

Sometimes it's a good idea to pick a cooking method to match your mood. Grilling is just right when you need action—hauling and lighting and brushing and, in my case, running up and down the back stairs. Pan-roasting fosters crisp textures and is very direct and efficient, ideal when you need something straightforward. Poaching is a gentler method for a more contemplative mood. You make a beautiful broth that makes the kitchen smell delicious and let the fish bathe in it until it's done. It feels deliberate and restorative at once.

Meat Loaf for Sandwiches

Makes 8 sandwiches

I really don't ever serve meat loaf as meat loaf. It would be delicious warm with some roasted veggies on the side and a good grainy mustard. But I make my meat loaf in anticipation of the most delicious sandwiches, like a lower-effort pâté of sorts that shines with soft-centered white bread and a leaf or two of extra-crunchy lettuce (see Note). I do like to layer a lot of flavors into my meat loaf, like orange peel, red wine, anchovies, chile, and pecorino—so have some fun with the construction of this lovely loaf.

Olive oil

Grated zest of ½ orange

2 cups (480 ml) dry red wine

¾ cup (180 ml) tomato passata

6 anchovies

Pinch of red chile flakes

1 clove garlic, peeled

1 pound (455 g) ground pork

1 pound (455 g) ground turkey

1 pound (455 g) ground beef

1½ cups (90 g) Plain Dried Breadcrumbs (page 26)

3 ounces (85 g) pecorino Romano cheese, grated

2 teaspoons sea salt, plus more to top

Lots of freshly ground black pepper

2 cloves garlic, grated

2 large eggs, lightly beaten

3 ounces (85 g) basil leaves, no stems

Preheat the oven to 375°F (190°C). Lightly grease a 9 × 5 × 3-inch (23 × 12 × 8 cm) loaf pan with olive oil.

In a blender, combine the orange zest, 1 cup (240 ml) of the red wine, the tomato passata, anchovies, chile flakes, and garlic. Blend until pureed.

In a large bowl, combine the ground pork, turkey, and beef. Sprinkle in half of the breadcrumbs, then add the cheese, salt, pepper, garlic, and eggs. Using your fingers as a rake, combine everything together until well blended.

Pack half of the meat mixture into the bottom of the prepared loaf pan. Pour in the tomato mixture. Place the basil leaves in a single layer atop the tomato mixture. Cover with the remaining meat mixture and gently spread from edge to edge of the pan, being careful not to squish out the tomato layer. Sprinkle about half of the remaining breadcrumbs across the meat loaf, then drizzle the remaining 1 cup (240 ml) wine across the whole meat loaf. Finally, use the remaining breadcrumbs to cover the whole top of the loaf. Season the top of the meat loaf with salt and pepper.

Set the loaf pan on a sheet pan and cook the meat loaf to an internal temperature of 155 to 160°F (68 to 71°C), 60 to 70 minutes.

(Recipe continues)

Serve right away, or if moving onto sandwiches (see Note), let cool to room temperature, then refrigerate overnight.

Note: I can't quite bring myself to write a full recipe for a meat loaf sandwich, but as with all sandwiches, the details add up to make them special: I start with sliced white bread from our local bakery, Sea Wolf, cut ¾-inch (2 cm) thick, lightly toasted. Spread a little too much mayonnaise on one side of the bread, making sure to get to all the edges. On the other piece of bread, spread a thin layer of Dijon mustard. Place a big hunk of room-temperature meat loaf, about ¾ inch (2 cm) thick, on the mayonnaise. Then lay a couple of ribs from the inside of a head of romaine on top of that. Finally, top with the mustardy bread slice. Eat it with both hands, and if you are like my husband, Dan, you won't put it down until you're finished.

Vegetables Are Remarkable

Mixed Media from the Garden

When I first started cooking professionally, vegetables were very much just there to goose up the meat or the fish at the center of the plate, but, of course, the food world has changed on that subject. Now vegetables are very much accepted as the kitchen stars that they are, and we embrace them at every delicious stage of their life cycle: flowering blossoms from over-wintered kale, the first tiny spring radishes, squash blossoms, young, crisp zucchini, and weighty winter root vegetables. Vegetables are just as full of flavorful and poetic potential as any other ingredient.

They take me back to fleeting pleasures like the times, as a kid, I was sent off to the garden to weed. Who could focus on a messy task when there were warm, fresh peas on the vine? I'd forget about the knotweed and instead I'd pick a pod, open it like a book, and pluck pea by pea from the glossy interior. Then I'd do it again. My dog Lamont had a similar approach to the garden and would carefully purse his whiskered lips to pluck raspberries, one at a time, from the cane.

These days I don't mind weeding so much, but I still snack along the way, nibbling on spicy arugula flowers and young fava pods as I dig. The garden is a spot I go to for calm and creativity, and not just kitchen creativity. I process my way through work and family dilemmas as I pluck out the stray weeds. I plan weekend trips, and I get inspired to make paintings. To my mind, there are few better painting subjects than a ripe tomato, a curling cucumber vine, or a growing pumpkin just blushing orange after a green summer.

Cooking vegetables is such a good creative challenge—I try to determine how best to celebrate the ephemeral moment when each vegetable is at its peak. And my CSA box full of mixed vegetables is a constant prompt to showcase them in the best ways. The goal of a good vegetable dish is to frame the ingredients, transforming them just enough but not obliterating their individual characteristics. That might mean browning cauliflower to the edge of being burnt to emphasize the contrast between its craggy florets and the soft, fragrant interior. Other times, I shoot for complete silkiness, like my simple braised zucchini (page 108)

that is practically a zucchini jam after its long stewing in olive oil. And then other times completely raw is the way to go—a quick salt cure on a big tangle of winter vegetables makes a colorful slaw a bit more tender while holding on to a satisfying crunch.

I think back to those college studio days and how different it felt to draw with fine pen tips one day and another with chunky hunks of charcoal. Each tool dictated a different kind of storytelling, in scale, in detail, even how long it took to finish a work. It's not that different when cooking with vegetables—a creative cook can have an intention for a dish, but also must be responsive to the way the media wants to behave. In the vegetable world, nothing is completely uniform in shape, texture, size, or even humidity, and these characteristics reward careful observation and flexibility on the part of the cook. Sometimes those potatoes are going to take longer to cook than others. You might need to trim some blemishes from an otherwise gorgeous batch of green beans. You might need to soak a few lettuce leaves in icy water to crisp them up after sitting in the fridge a little too long. I hope this book can challenge you as a cook to use your senses to see when things are ready: sniffing, poking, tasting for what is just the right preparation for you.

CSA Slaw with Cabbage, Beet, and Celery Root

Serves 4 to 6

If you have ever gotten a CSA subscription, you know that feeling when you get a slightly random one or two of everything from your farmer. One move is to make minestrone or some other veggie soup, but I also like to shred everything finely on a mandoline (using the finger guard!) and craft a wonderfully bright, limey salad, showered with crunchy nuts and sesame seeds. Here I lay out the basic structure, but if you got a kohlrabi or a daikon instead, you know what to do. Enjoy the improvisation. If you are feeling even more ambitious, serve it with a batch of Grilled Sesame Flatbread (page 50).

1⅔ cups/8 ounces (225 g) whole almonds

½ medium white cabbage

2 teaspoons salt

2 large golden beets (about 18 ounces/500 g)

1 small celery root (about 7 ounces/200 g)

2 to 3 large carrots (about 12 ounces/340 g)

Grated zest and juice of 3 limes

1 cup (240 ml) plain yogurt

¼ cup (60 ml) olive oil, plus more to serve

1 clove garlic, grated

1 teaspoon za'atar

Freshly ground black pepper

½ cup (75 g) toasted sesame seeds

1 packed cup (60 g) dill fronds, lightly chopped

1 packed cup (60 g) mint leaves, lightly chopped

Flaky salt, to serve

Fancy olive oil, to serve

Preheat the oven to 350°F (175°C).

Lay the almonds on a sheet pan and toast them until they start to crack. Watch them closely: About 9 minutes in, I usually bite into one to see if it's no longer white on the inside. When toasted, remove from the oven and let cool to room temperature, then crush in a mortar and pestle or coarsely chop.

Slice the cabbage on a mandoline into a large bowl. Sprinkle on 1 teaspoon of the fine sea salt and mix by hand well, massaging the salt into the cabbage. Next, prepare the beets, celery root, and carrots by slicing them thinly on a mandoline and then slicing the pieces into thin julienned strips. Mix each vegetable into the cabbage as you finish slicing it, tossing and squeezing with your hands to combine and distribute the salt. When the vegetable mixture has sat for 30 minutes to 1 hour, place in a colander and rinse quickly. Then lay the vegetables on a clean kitchen towel (not your fanciest one: the beets may leak a little color onto them) and blot well (maybe using a second towel to really get the moisture off).

In a small bowl, make the dressing by whisking together the lime zest and juice, yogurt, olive oil, garlic, za'atar, and remaining 1 teaspoon fine sea salt. Season well with pepper. Taste and adjust the salt if necessary.

(Recipe continues)

Transfer the vegetables to a large bowl and fold in the yogurt dressing and most of the almonds, sesame seeds, dill, and mint, reserving some for the top of the salad. Pile the salad onto a serving platter or bowl and scatter the remaining sesame seeds, almonds, and herbs over the top. Drizzle with some olive oil and sprinkle with flaky salt.

Work in Progress: Midwinter Color

Earlier in this book I wrote in praise of plain brown food (see page 82). But I also can lean into a dish like this that has just about every color happening at once. Color is such an important component of food, especially in winter. A vibrant dish is visually invigorating—a little edible reassurance that that color will return to the world after winter's darkness. And it is also a great balance to that brown beef stew you might be serving alongside it.

Charred Eggplant with Romesco

Serves 4 to 6

I think eggplant is best when it has a chance to get a little charred and smoky, as in this simple preparation. Timing can vary a bit, since eggplants vary in size and density, but you are looking to get them dark golden brown on their cut surfaces and completely yielding and tender at their interiors. My variation on the nutty Catalan pepper sauce romesco is a wonderfully tangy partner for the smoky eggplant. There's one more little special accent here: When my garden cilantro bolts and flowers, the leaves get more pungent, but there is a happy consequence: fresh coriander seeds that are herbaceous and lemony and very pretty. If you have some unruly cilantro plants on hand, by all means, grab some of the little green seeds and use them as a garnish for this dish. If not, dried coriander seeds, quickly crushed with a mortar and pestle, are lovely too.

3 pounds (1.4 kg) eggplant

3 tablespoons olive oil, plus more for greasing

Salt

1 tablespoon coriander seeds, fresh if possible, lightly crushed with a mortar and pestle

Romesco Sauce (recipe follows)

Flaky salt, to finish

2 tablespoons fresh cilantro leaves, torn

Fresh coriander flowers (optional)

Cut the eggplants in half, top to bottom. Rub them with olive oil and coat evenly, then season with fine sea salt.

Prepare a grill to medium-high heat. Clean the grates well. Lay the eggplants cut side down on the grill and cook until richly browned. Turn the eggplant and cook until very tender and collapsing, 15 to 20 minutes, depending on their size. (Check them regularly because different eggplants may have slightly different cooking times.) When done, they will be dark in color, the skin will blister, and they will steam out of the cut side. Remove the eggplant from the grill and let it rest for 10 minutes.

In a small bowl, stir the coriander seeds into the olive oil.

Cut each eggplant piece lengthwise down the middle and peel off as much skin as possible. Spoon about 2 cups of the romesco on a serving platter. Pile the cooked eggplant on top of the romesco. Spoon the coriander seeds and oil atop the eggplant. Garnish with flaky salt and a sprinkle of cilantro leaves.

Romesco Sauce

Makes about 3 cups (720 ml)

⅓ cup (75 ml) plus up to ¼ cup (60 ml) olive oil

⅔ cup (90 g) hazelnuts

3 cloves garlic, sliced

2 Fresno chiles, seeded and chopped

2 tablespoons sweet paprika

2 teaspoons salt, plus more as needed

1 (12-ounce/340 g) jar roasted red peppers, drained and coarsely chopped

¼ cup (60 ml) sherry vinegar (I love Arvum Vinagre de Jerez)

Put ⅓ cup (75 ml) of the olive oil, the hazelnuts, garlic, and chiles in a large skillet over medium heat. Stir in the paprika and salt. Cook until the garlic is lightly browned and fragrant, about 4 minutes.

Place the contents of the skillet in a food processor and add the roasted peppers and vinegar along with 2 tablespoons olive oil. Process into a chunky smooth puree. If possible, let sit for 1 hour at room temperature before serving. Check the seasoning and add more salt if necessary and additional olive oil if needed to make a nice spoonable texture. It will keep for at least 2 days in an airtight container in the refrigerator.

Mushroom Duxelles on Olive Oil–Soaked, Garlic-Rubbed Toast

Serves 4

Mushroom duxelles—a butter mushroom spread—is at the top of the chart of brownest foods, right up there with beef stew and chopped liver. And like those other two, it makes up in flavor for what it lacks in vivid color. You don't need fancy mushrooms to make a duxelles, though if you have some on hand after a foraging trip, please go for it! I usually choose a mix of the nice grocery-store varieties—some buttons or cremini, some oysters, maybe a king oyster or two. Duxelles is an excellent snack to have on hand when friends show up for dinner.

1½ pounds (680 g) assorted mushrooms, tough stems trimmed

1 tablespoon minced thyme leaves and tender stems

3 tablespoons unsalted butter

1 shallot, finely minced

1 clove garlic, finely minced, plus 1 clove, peeled, to serve

Salt and freshly ground black pepper

Grated zest of 1 lemon

2 tablespoons dry sherry

Pinch of red chile flakes

Thick-sliced sourdough bread, to serve

Fancy olive oil, to serve

Small handful fresh basil leaves (purple if available), to serve

In a food processor fitted with a steel blade, process the mushrooms with the thyme until the mushrooms are finely and evenly chopped.

In a large sauté pan over medium-high heat, melt the butter. Add the mushroom mixture, shallot, and minced garlic and turn the heat down to medium. Cook, stirring occasionally, for 1 to 2 minutes. Season with salt and pepper and keep cooking: The mushrooms will gradually release their water.

When the mixture is pretty dry, another 1 to 2 minutes, add the lemon zest, sherry, and chile flakes. Turn the heat down to medium-low and cook for 10 to 12 minutes, stirring frequently, until the mushrooms have released and cooked off their liquid and are a slightly darker shade of brown. If the mushrooms start to stick to the bottom of the pan, you can add 1 to 2 tablespoons water and stir to scrape up any sticky bits. Remove from the heat and let cool. The duxelles can be cooked a day or two ahead and stored in the refrigerator. Make sure to bring to room temperature or warmer before serving.

Toast the bread, and as you remove the slices from the toaster, rub them with the garlic clove. Drizzle the toast with olive oil, spread a nice layer of the duxelles on the toast, and serve topped with basil leaves.

Ready to roast cauliflower

Eggplant ready for the grill

farmers' Market fennel

Almost-Burnt Cauliflower with Yogurt, Lime Peel, and Urfa Biber

Serves 4 to 6

This recipe is a kind of a dare: How charred and crispy can I get the leaves and edges of that cauliflower before it becomes a scorched mess? I'll let you play the game too—don't get scared off too early, because the caramelized edges on the cauliflower bring out a funky sweetness. I used miniature heads of purple cauliflower, so the result was extra dark, but you can use whatever is most fetching in your market: purple, white, or orange cauliflower would all work wonderfully.

Rounded ½ cup/3 ounces (85 g) skin-on almonds

2½ pounds (1.2 kg) cauliflower (about 1 very large cauliflower)

¼ cup (60 ml) olive oil

1½ teaspoons salt, plus more as needed

16 ounces (480 ml) sheep's milk yogurt

Grated zest of 1 lime

1 clove garlic, grated

2 tablespoons urfa biber pepper flakes (see Note)

Lime wedges, to serve

Place one shelf in the center of the oven and another on the top slot of the oven and preheat to 350°F (175°C).

Lay the almonds on a sheet pan and place in the oven on the center rack. Toast, shaking occasionally, until the almonds are quite browned at their centers and the skins are loosened, about 15 minutes. Remove from the oven and increase the oven temperature to 425°C (220°C). Cool the nuts, then coarsely chop them.

Cut the cauliflower into 3-inch (7.5 cm) wedges (try to keep some flat surfaces to allow nice browning on the sheet pan. In a large bowl, toss the cauliflower wedges with the olive oil and 1 teaspoon of the salt.

Lay the cauliflower wedges on a sheet pan, drizzle the olive oil on both sides, and roast for about 20 minutes, until browned on the bottom: A knife inserted into the thick stem of the cauliflower should go in easily. Flip the cauliflower wedges over, rotate the pan, place back in the oven, and roast for 5 minutes. Start the broiler, move the sheet pan to the top shelf, and broil for 3 to 4 minutes, until most of the edges and leaves of the cauliflower are dark brown and crispy. The more you are willing to push the color, the more exciting the texture will be. If a few pieces are getting browned faster than others, you

(Recipe continues)

can carefully remove them to a serving plate with tongs and return the pan under the broiler. Watch carefully, as broilers vary considerably.

While the cauliflower is roasting, stir together the yogurt, grated lime zest, the remaining ½ teaspoon salt, and the grated garlic in a medium bowl. Taste the sauce and adjust with more salt if necessary. Chill until ready to serve.

To serve, spoon the sauce generously at the base of the serving platter. Pile on the charred cauliflower, sprinkle with urfa biber pepper flakes, and finish with a squeeze from the lime wedges. Top with the toasted almonds and serve with the lime wedges.

Note: One key flavor here is the almost meaty taste of dark-cured, not-too-hot Turkish pepper flakes known as urfa biber. You can order urfa biber from Villa Jerada (and other wonderful spice houses).

Work in Progress: Texture as a Creative Tool

The crispy little edges in food are one of the great pleasures in life—both texture and flavor become more interesting with a bit of blistering and caramelization. And so, it's fun to play with the grill or the broiler or the grill pan to manipulate a favorite dish a bit. There is such a thing as too burnt: see the recent trends for absolutely charred Basque cheesecake and little piles of burnt vegetable ash on the margins of plates, or the last time I walked away from my sourdough loaves in the backyard wood oven! But exploring the range of caramelization from pale straw gold to the darkest black-brown edges on a barbecued rib—well that is one of the things that keeps me fully engaged when I am cooking.

Roasted Castelfranco with Soft Scrambled Eggs, Parmigiano, and Balsamic Vinegar

Serves 2

I am so smitten with the spectrum of chicories—Italian bitter green and cream and red leafy vegetables—that I can now find in Seattle from late summer until early spring. This dish, made with the gorgeously speckled radicchio variety Castelfranco, is the perfect dinner night in with your sweetheart. If you can't get Castelfranco, regular radicchio, Treviso, or a smallish escarole is a good substitute. The bitterness of the leaves is cushioned by the soft luxury of the eggs and a kiss of sweet-tart balsamic vinegar. (A request: Please spend some good money on your balsamic—you don't need to get extravagant condiment grade, but invest enough to get barrel-aged vinegar—it will last nearly forever in the fridge and you only need a bit at a time. Typical grocery store balsamic is too thin and sour and lacks the resonance of traditional balsamic.) The dish comes together quickly after you add the eggs, so have your serving plates warm and your guest in the room and ready to eat. Dan is, fortunately, almost always ready to eat. Serve with a plate of prosciutto di Parma and pretend you are in Parma, Italy.

1 Castelfranco radicchio, about 7 ounces (200 g)

4 tablespoons (60 ml) olive oil

Salt and freshly ground black pepper

4 large eggs, whisked and seasoned with salt and pepper

½ cup (65 g) grated Parmigiano-Reggiano cheese

Excellent-quality balsamic vinegar (I like Chiarli)

Before cooking, cut each Castelfranco in half top to bottom and then again to make 4 quarters. Trim away three-quarters of the thick core in the middle of each Castelfranco wedge. It will cook more evenly this way. You're looking for wedges no more than 1 inch (2.5 cm) thick, so bigger chicories may need to be cut more.

Heat 2 tablespoons of the olive oil in a large steel pan over medium heat. When shimmering, place the cut Castelfranco wedges cut side down in the pan, leaving a couple of inches between each piece (depending on the size of the pan, you may need to work in two batches). After about 2 minutes, flip each wedge and season with a bit of salt and pepper. Cook for another 2 minutes, removing any single leaves as they look done; it is nice to get a bit of browning on the wedges. Remove the wedges to a nearby plate and set aside.

(Recipe continues)

Add the remaining 2 tablespoons olive oil to the pan and increase the heat to medium-high. Stir half of the cheese into the seasoned eggs. When the oil is shimmering, pour in the eggs; they will cook quickly, so be ready! As soon as the eggs set a bit, give them a quick scramble with a spatula, then add the cooked chicories. Fold the mixture once, then turn the heat off.

At this point you can remove it or leave it in the pan to cook with residual heat until the eggs are set to your preference—I like my scrambles soft. Plate with the rest of the cheese, a bit more black pepper, and a generous drizzle of fancy balsamic vinegar. Eat right away.

Green Beans with Crème Fraîche, Shallot, and Dijon Vinaigrette

Serves 4 to 6

My mom was and is still a great bean gardener, setting up elegant wooden stake tipis to support her Blue Lake vines. The resulting beans are so succulent. Meanwhile, last year I grew my pole beans on the skeleton of an old outdoor umbrella—a much clunkier solution. It's always good to know the elements of your kitchen palette that are guaranteed to delight you. Here are three of my favorites: Dijon mustard, tarragon, and crème fraîche. They unite to deliver a pure summer delight: a tart, smooth, and fragrant dressing for a pile of crunchy-tender blanched green beans.

1 tablespoon unsalted butter

3 shallots, minced (about ½ cup/60 g)

2 heaping tablespoons Dijon mustard

Grated zest of 1 large lemon

4 tablespoons (60 ml) lemon juice

1 teaspoon champagne or other white wine vinegar

¼ cup (60 ml) olive oil

8 ounces (240 ml) crème fraîche

1 teaspoon salt, plus more as needed

Lots of freshly ground black pepper

1½ pounds (680 g) green beans, left whole, stems removed

½ cup (26 g) chopped tarragon leaves

Mini marigold flowers or other edible flowers, for garnish (optional)

Place the butter and minced shallots in a medium saucepan and melt the butter over medium-low heat, 1 to 2 minutes, allowing the shallots to soften. Remove from the heat and whisk in the mustard, lemon zest and juice, vinegar, olive oil, and crème fraîche. Season with the salt and lots of black pepper. Taste and adjust the salt if necessary. Set the mixture aside.

Bring a large stockpot of salted water to a rolling boil. Have ready a large mixing bowl full of ice water and a sheet pan lined with a double layer of paper towels. When the water boils, drop in the beans all at once and cook until they are tender but retain a bit of a bite, about 4 minutes. Lift the beans out of the pot and shock them in the ice water. When cold, drain them and lay them out on the paper towels. When dry, dress the beans with the crème fraîche mixture. Fold in the tarragon leaves and pile the beans on a serving plate with edible flowers (if using).

Work in Progress: Developing a Flavor Palette

Part of developing kitchen confidence is knowing what will always make you excited to eat or serve something. In my green bean recipe, I use some deep-down favorite flavors like tarragon, mustard, and crème fraîche. Experimentation is an important part of my creative process, but so is gathering my favorite palette of flavors, which give me great confidence.

Cauliflower Gratin with Nutmeg and Gruyère

Serves 4 to 6

If you ever want to make a vegetable dish with real presence, a gratin is a great choice: browned and crusty on top, supple and creamy inside. I love to make gratins with potatoes, kale, endive, you name it. This variation is an old favorite with an ingredient list that is almost austere: just cauliflower, cream, cheese, and a few spices. Simple as it is, it is so silky and delicious in a pretty shade of winter white, offset with a rich, amber crust. It may be my favorite of all gratins.

4 to 5 pounds (1.8 to 2.3 kg) cauliflower, about 2 medium heads, trimmed and cut into florets

¾ cup (180 ml) heavy cream, plus more if needed

A few fresh gratings of nutmeg

Pinch of cayenne pepper

2 teaspoons salt

¾ cup (75 g) grated Gruyère cheese

Preheat the oven to 375°F (190°C). Have ready a 9 × 13-inch (23 × 33 cm) baking dish or one of similar volume.

Set up a large pot with a steamer basket and fill it with as much water as can fit without touching the bottom of the basket. Put the cauliflower in the basket, bring the water to a boil, and when it begins to steam, cover the pot and steam the cauliflower until it is very tender and yielding, 12 to 14 minutes. Carefully remove the cauliflower from the steamer and transfer to the bowl of a food processor fitted with a metal blade. Add the cream, nutmeg, cayenne pepper, and salt. Process until very smooth, about 3 minutes; you want the mixture to be a little more fluid than mashed potatoes. If it is still stiff, add more cream a couple of tablespoons at a time. Taste and adjust the salt if desired.

Scrape the mixture into the prepared baking dish. Cover the top evenly with the cheese and place in the oven. Bake until bubbly and browned, about 45 minutes. Let it cool just a touch and serve.

Lettuces with Soft-Boiled Egg, Toasted Pecans, and Tahini-Tarragon Dressing

Serves 4 to 6

My friend Carrie's beautiful giant purple lettuces were so full and lush they looked like huge peonies. I designed a salad around them that is a satisfying dinner—eggs, nuts, radishes, and a richer dressing. All it needed was wine and good bread, enough for a meal. Any leftover dressing is great to dip bread into or for a salad the next day.

6 large eggs

½ cup (120 ml) tahini (I like the Villa Jerada brand)

3 tablespoons olive oil

1 clove garlic, peeled

½ cup (120 ml) plain whole-milk yogurt

3 tablespoons lemon juice

1 cup (60 g) picked loosely packed tarragon leaves

½ teaspoon honey

Salt and freshly ground black pepper

1 large butter or bibb lettuce (about 1¾ pounds/800 g), leaves separated

6 radishes, sliced into very thin coins with a mandoline

1 cup (120 g) toasted pecans

Have a big bowl of ice and water prepared. Bring a 3- to 4-quart (2.8 to 3.8 liter) pot of water to a boil over high heat. Gently lower the eggs into the water and turn down the heat to maintain a gentle simmer. Cook for 6½ minutes, then remove the eggs directly to the ice bath. Peel as soon as they are cool enough to handle. The eggs could be cooked the day before you want to make the salad.

Prepare the dressing: In a blender, combine the tahini, olive oil, garlic, yogurt, lemon juice, tarragon, and honey. Blend until very smooth and creamy. Thin with a little bit of water if needed and season well with salt and pepper.

Layer the lettuce on a deep platter, followed by the eggs, radishes, a liberal amount of the dressing (you should have about ½ cup/120 ml left over), then the pecans, and serve. Store the leftover dressing in an airtight container in the fridge for up to 3 days.

Spring Onion Tart with Chèvre, Dill, and Black Pepper

Serves 4

My mom always made quiche with little bits of leftovers. The classic was ham and cheese, but snippets of veggies would make their way in too. I still like to incorporate veggie odds and ends into my savory tarts— a handful of peas, a pint of mushrooms, or turnip tops from a CSA haul. This tart is a bit shallower than my mom's quiches, with an extra-crispy shell that's prebaked before filling and baking again. I made this version with long spring onions that are one of the first real veggies to make it into the markets in the Seattle spring. By that time of the year, we are all dying for something fresh, so hallelujah, little onions!

1 batch Savory Tart Crust (recipe follows)

2 tablespoons unsalted butter

10 spring onions, sliced in half lengthwise, root ends trimmed but core intact

1 cup (240 ml) heavy cream

3 large eggs

1½ teaspoons salt, plus more as needed

½ cup (25 g) packed dill fronds (no stems), lightly chopped

Freshly ground black pepper

4 ounces (115 g) fresh chèvre

Preheat the oven to 400°F (205°C).

Roll the tart dough out to ⅛ inch (3 mm) and carefully lay it into a 9½-inch (24 cm) tart pan, lifting the dough and gently poking it into the edges of the pan. Fold the edge of the dough over the top of the pan and crimp. Line the dough with parchment paper. Fold it to lightly cover the rim of the dough, then secure it with pie weights or a couple of cups of dried beans. Bake the shell until it is dry, 15 to 20 minutes, then remove the parchment and weights and bake for another 5 minutes, or until the shell is a bit golden.

While the shell is baking, prepare the filling. In a large skillet over medium heat, melt the butter. Place the spring onions in the pan cut side down and gently cook, turning occasionally, until the onions are softened and slightly translucent, 8 to 10 minutes.

In a medium bowl, whisk together the cream, eggs, and salt until smooth.

When the shell is finished baking, spread the cooked onions evenly across it and sprinkle with about half of the dill and a few cracks of black pepper. Spread the chèvre crumbles evenly across the tart. Pour in the egg mixture and finish with the rest of the dill.

Place in the oven and bake until the custard is gently set, about 30 minutes.

Let cool for at least 10 minutes before serving warm. The tart can also be served at room temperature.

Savory Tart Crust

Makes one 9½-inch (24 cm) tart crust

Savory tart dough in the freezer makes you feel prepared for seasonal inspiration.

1½ cups (185 g) all-purpose flour

1 teaspoon salt

4 tablespoons unsalted butter, very cold, cut into ½-inch (12 mm) chunks

¼ cup (60 ml) icy-cold water (maybe a touch more)

In a food processor, pulse together the flour and salt until combined. Add the butter and pulse until the butter is largely cornmeal-textured with some larger pea-sized chunks. Pulse and add a bit of the cold water at a time through the hole in the lid until the dough comes together.

Gather the dough together in a ball, wrap with parchment, then smoosh down into a neat disk. Refrigerate for at least 1 hour. It can be made ahead and kept in the fridge for 2 to 3 days or frozen for up to 1 month. If frozen, defrost in the refrigerator a day in advance. Take the dough out of the refrigerator 30 minutes before rolling.

Work in Progress: Don't Fear Repetition

In today's culture, there's a lot of pressure to present new things all the time. But as I've gotten more experience, I've gotten more comfortable with less novelty and more repetition of a favorite ingredient. While it's in season, I'll explore its textures and flavors in different preparations: I think of it as edible themes and variations. When spring onions are around, I want to use them a lot: in a tart, grilled up next to a steak, slivered in fried rice, whizzed into a green sauce. After their season I'll move on to other pet ingredients.

I ♥ chicories

After dinner loveliness

Spring onions for my tart

Tribute to Mom's Potato Salad

Serves 4 to 6

This is a riff on my mom's classic American potato salad, which she would have ready to go in a Tupperware in the fridge practically all summer long. Her version would be made with chopped pickles, egg, and yellow mustard (or maybe, on a fancy day, Gulden's), and it would go with the hamburgers, grilled salmon, and crab melts that I still dream about. In my version, I add a more charismatic mustard and my usual tornado of French-y herbs, but I keep the mayo. I'm happy with this salad living in the in-between space between French and American picnics.

2 pounds (910 g) small Yukon Gold potatoes

1½ teaspoons salt, plus more for the cooking water

¼ cup (60 ml) mayonnaise

2 tablespoons grainy mustard

¼ cup (60 ml) olive oil

1 tablespoon apple cider vinegar

Freshly ground black pepper

½ red onion, thinly sliced

1 cup (60 g) Italian parsley leaves, chopped

¼ cup (15 g) tarragon leaves, chopped

½ cup (25 g) minced chives

Place the potatoes in a large saucepan and cover with water. Salt the water and bring to a boil. Turn the heat down to maintain a simmer and cook until the potatoes are tender when poked with a knife. Drain. When cool enough to touch, chop the potatoes in half or quarter them and place in a large bowl.

In a small bowl, whisk together the mayonnaise, mustard, olive oil, and vinegar. Season the dressing with the salt and tons of black pepper.

Fold the dressing into the warm potatoes a little at a time until dressed to your taste. Sometimes potatoes are thirsty and need more dressing than others. Let cool for 15 minutes, then fold in the red onions, parsley, tarragon, and chives.

Winter Wedge with Cabbage, Stilton, and Dates

Serves 4 to 6

This roasted salad is a different kind of cabbage salad from the slaw earlier in this chapter (see page 134). Lots of cooked winter vegetables that are lean, sweet, and soft, like beets, squash, and carrots. That may be why I love cabbage so much, especially at the tail end of winter, when I'm impatient for fresh new flavors to come in at the market. Unlike those other winter standbys, cabbage is bracing and full of texture. If it's not cooked too long, it keeps its crunch and a little bright zinginess. This method—blasting it in the oven so its edges crisp and brown—well, it's my favorite because it maximizes textural contrast and it doesn't take much effort. As usual for me, it's all about contrast; this time between the crackly leaves, the creaminess of a warm blue cheese dressing, and the supple denseness of slivered dates.

2 cups (about 8 ounces/225 g) pitted Medjool dates, each sliced lengthwise into 3 slivers

1 cup (60 g) picked cilantro leaves

½ cup (120 ml) olive oil

1 teaspoon salt, plus more as needed

Finely grated zest of 1 Meyer lemon

3 tablespoons Meyer lemon juice

Freshly ground black pepper

1 Savoy cabbage, about 2 pounds (910 g), cut into 6 wedges

6 ounces (170 g) Stilton cheese

3 tablespoons heavy cream

Preheat the oven to 400°F (205°C).

In a small bowl, toss together the dates, cilantro, ¼ cup (60 ml) of the olive oil, the salt, lemon zest, and 2 tablespoons of the lemon juice. Season generously with pepper. Set aside.

Drizzle the remaining ¼ cup (60 ml) olive oil all over the sides of the cabbage wedges and place cut side down on a sheet pan. Season with salt. Roast in the oven, using a spatula to carefully flip each wedge after about 15 minutes. Keep roasting for another 20 to 25 minutes, until there is dark color at the cut edges and the stem is tender when poked with a small knife.

When the cabbage is ready, place a medium skillet over medium-low heat. Add the cheese and cream and cook, stirring often, until the cheese is melted. Remove the pan from the heat and whisk in the remaining 1 tablespoon lemon juice and a generous grinding of black pepper. Place the roasted cabbage on the serving platter and drizzle with the Stilton sauce. Top with a generous amount of black pepper and tuck the sliced dates all through the cabbage.

Everything Tastes Better Outdoors

Sunlight, Nostalgia, and Gratitude

Sunlight is a powerful condiment, and eating outdoors is just about my favorite thing. When I eat at the beach or on the back patio, I often find myself able to look at the meal with fondness as if it's already a memory. It's a feeling to cherish. This rush of nostalgia is probably tied to my childhood of summer meals eaten on the deck at my family's cabin at Spee-bi-dah, just off the Tulalip reservation on the Salish Sea north of Seattle.

At the cabin, we would walk down the beach to buy salmon from the Tulalip fishermen, just before they headed home at the end of their workday. We'd walk back home with the fish held hanging between us on a piece of driftwood. Once home we would scale and gut and fillet the fish on the picnic bench under the shade of the big-leaf maple tree, getting it ready for the grill. Sometimes a stray transparent scale would stick to my hand and glimmer like a sequin in the late-afternoon light. Mom would just slather on mayonnaise and grill the salmon until it was bubbly with a gorgeous amber crust. We'd keep everything else simple to go with the incredible fish: things like sliced tomatoes from one of the pots on the terrace or potato salad made with baby red potatoes and bound together with yet more mayo (see page 162). Being outdoors at the beach or in my garden always reminds me of where our ingredients are coming from, and all they need is the slightest boost to lift them up for a celebration. The rules and the expectations all feel a little looser when making food outside.

I do like to be near a kitchen or another cooking source when I eat outside. In other words, I am not a true picnicker—I don't want to pack it all up! My more elaborate outdoor meals stay close to a kitchen or an outdoor oven or barbecue. The process of tending a fire or settling a cast-iron pan into a bed of coals is part of the joy of eating outdoors to me. If I do head out for a day of spot-prawn fishing on the boat, I tend to just bring snacks like salami and cheese, and of course a knife and a small bottle of olive oil and a lime for when we catch our shrimp and want to have a little prawn crudo on board!

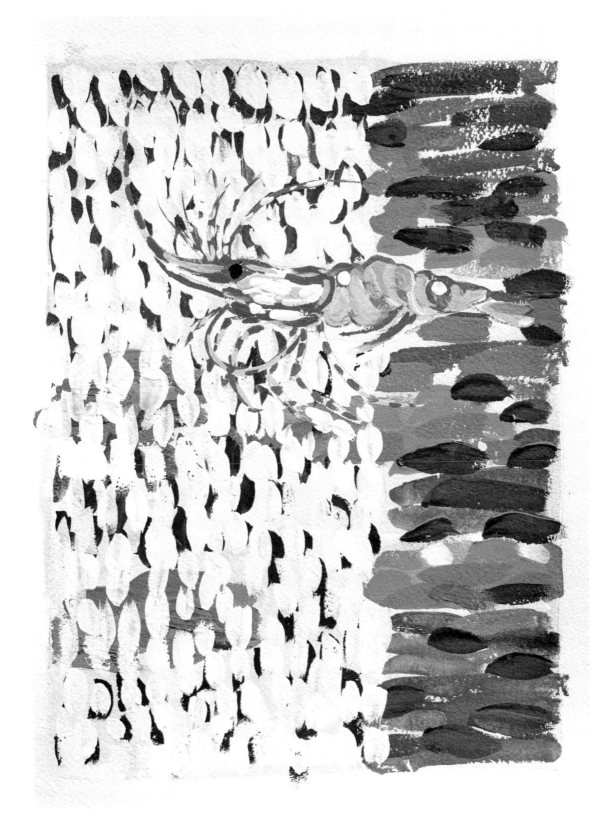

I still join my parents up at their cabin, and I love to barbecue oysters on the Hood Canal or grill with my friends on Vashon Island. But the best outdoors is the one you can get to most easily: These days I most often eat outside in my own backyard, where Dan built me a brick pizza oven a couple of years ago. Of course, I make pizzas, but I also use it to roast market vegetables and big hunks of lamb. While things are in the oven, I love to paint outdoors: The bright lighting reminds me that the natural palette isn't at all restrained! There's the lurid pink interior of green-skinned figs just off the tree, the flashy silver salmon skin, the hot tangerine of nasturtiums, and the searing blue of the August sky.

Over the past few years, I have become more serious about photography (for the first time, I am shooting the images in my own cookbook!), and that creative process has made me appreciate eating outdoors all the more. I love to see the way a leafy tree breaks up the morning light on a slice of summer coffee cake, or how the last coral rays of sun skim across a melon salad on a summer-twilight dinner. Even without a camera in hand, the moment of pause to take in the light makes me grateful for each moment I have around the table.

My gratitude for being outside and the rich ingredients I've been able to choose here in the Pacific Northwest have propelled me to make some hard choices about sourcing for myself and my restaurants. As the environmental conditions and our knowledge of threats to our natural world evolve, I have tried to make better choices for a sustainable future (and I am trying hard to help encourage you to do the same). We do our best to supply the restaurants with regionally grown products (like Billy's luscious tomatoes and exquisite chicories from farms like Local Roots). Seafood is a trickier field to navigate. We have all but eliminated open ocean–caught fish from our menus. We've scrubbed our kitchens of customer-favorite king (Chinook) salmon because they are also the primary food source for threatened southern resident orcas. At the same time, we are promoting sockeye and pink salmon. These are fished in more responsible ways, like place-based fisheries, where fish are trapped very selectively at the mouths of their natal rivers, giving the rest of their generation a better chance to return home to spawn. I have also used my outsized voice in the food industry to urge against open-water fish farming (which poses risks to native fish stocks and produces inferior fish) and pushed against the use of dangerous chemicals in shellfish farming.

The choices I make in my restaurants are not immaculate—we tried hard to eliminate the use of plastic wrap, for example, and still haven't found a workable alternative. But I do my best to honor the natural environment I grew up in—adapting our practices, making better choices when we can, and urging you, if you can afford it, to try to keep environmental pressures in mind as you shop for your dinner. And keep eating outside if you can! I think it will help remind you, as it does me, how delicate and inspiring the web of our food supply really is.

At this moment in history, we don't generally cook outdoors to make things simpler for ourselves. We do it to make a special moment to enjoy the world around us. In a way, cooking outdoors is a kind of performance—there's the lighting of the grill, the ferrying of supplies out from the car or the kitchen. There's the monitoring and turning of things on the grill and the arranging on the serving platter. Embrace this outdoor-cooking dance and invite your guests to be a part of it— they can grab herbs from the garden, help shuck the oysters, or just stand next to you with a glass of rosé and some good gossip as you grill.

A note on grilling: Of course, I do a lot of grilling when I am cooking outdoors. Here are a few tips that might help with your own grilling practice.

I don't use a gas grill, nor do I use lighter fluid—a charcoal chimney is just the right tool for me. Fill the top generously with hardwood charcoal—ideally the bigger chunks—before lighting the newspaper in the lower chamber. When you use a chimney, let the coals inside get red hot before emptying into the grill—depending on how fast you want to cook things, you can spread them out evenly or keep them in a pile for more intensity on one side of the grill (and a cooler spot to remove the ingredients to in case of flare-ups). Also remember to scour your grill grate both before placing ingredients on it and after you are done cooking—the heat and fire of the grill make it much easier to clean when it is warm. I grill year-round, and if I make a point of grilling in spring drizzle, then by summertime my technique is in really good shape. But grilling in the darker months can be tricky—you might want to add a lantern or flashlight to your grilling equipment so you can better monitor your cooking progress. Have that and everything you might need—including a glass of wine if you like—right near the grill. That means a chimney to start the coals, tongs, a clean plate for the finished dish, your brush if you are basting, a friend to chat with, etc. An always-helpful thermometer is even more useful in the off-season, as it's hard to judge doneness with less light. Remove the stress of having to run back inside for these things. Enjoy the outdoors, and remember, grilling is special.

Spicy Marinated Feta

Serves 4 to 6

Everything in this recipe is meant to be chunky and bold: The spices, lemon peel, and slivered chiles all bring not just big flavor but compelling texture to the feta. Salty and very tangy, feta can handle the bold accents. If you're up for a bit of a special project, try grilling sesame flatbread (page 50) to dip in the seasoned oil—it's such a big treat to have fresh bubbly bread still steaming from the grill, which you might have lit anyway if you're dining outdoors. But if you are in a rush, you can pair the marinated feta with any good bread.

2 teaspoons coriander seeds

1 teaspoon cumin seeds

1 pound (455 g) firm feta cheese, preferably sheep's milk, drained and cut into 1½-inch (4 cm) chunks

1 cup (240 ml) olive oil

2 serrano chiles, very thinly sliced (a mandoline works well)

Zest of 1 medium lemon, very thinly slivered

¼ cup (15 g) packed fresh mint leaves, torn into ½-inch (12 mm) pieces

1 heaping tablespoon marjoram leaves

1 batch Grilled Sesame Flatbread (page 50) or other good bread

In a dry skillet, toast the coriander and cumin seeds over medium-high heat until fragrant. Crush the seeds in a mortar and pestle or coarsely chop in a spice grinder.

In a medium bowl, combine the cheese, toasted spices, olive oil, chiles, and lemon zest. Store in an airtight container in the refrigerator for at least 8 hours or overnight. Flip the container occasionally or stir the contents every few hours to make sure the marinade is well distributed. The marinated cheese can be kept in an airtight container in the refrigerator for 2 to 3 days; if the cheese is poking out of the oil, add some more to the top to keep it submerged. Bring to room temperature before serving.

To serve, reserve a few herb leaves for garnish and then toss the rest of the mint and marjoram with the cheese. Arrange the cheese on a serving platter, spooning the chunky bits and oil over the top of the cheese. Top with the reserved mint and marjoram leaves and serve with warm bread.

Chunky Melon with Cucumber, Tarragon, and Whipped Ricotta

Serves 4 to 6

There is a time in the summer when you need to just eat all the juicy foods to cool off: watermelon, cantaloupe, cucumbers, and tomatoes take a huge slice of my bandwidth in summer, when I often wait until after our late sundown to eat dinner outside in the cooling light beneath the sunset. One recent August evening at my friends Andrew and Sara's Vashon Island house, we watched the golden gleam of sunlight sift out of the black water around ten p.m.! This salad, centered on an aromatic sunset-colored melon, is perfect for a dusky evening. It's soothing and sophisticated all at once.

2 cucumbers, peeled and seeded and cut into rustic 1- to 2-inch (2.5 to 5 cm) chunks

½ large orange-fleshed melon (orange honeydew, cantaloupe, or Charentais), cut into wedges and then into rustic 1- to 2-inch (2.5 cm to 5 cm) chunks

½ teaspoon freshly ground black pepper

1 teaspoon salt, plus more as needed

¼ cup (60 ml) olive oil, plus more to serve

1 tablespoon lemon juice

¾ cup (45 g) whole tarragon leaves

1 batch Whipped Ricotta (page 34), chilled for at least 45 minutes before assembly

Flaky salt, to serve

Chill a deep serving dish or bowl before getting to work.

In a large bowl, stir together the cucumbers, melon, black pepper, salt, olive oil, and lemon juice. Mix in the tarragon leaves and chill until ready to serve.

Spoon the whipped ricotta into the bottom of a deep serving dish or bowl. Pile the melon and cucumber mixture on top of the ricotta. Spoon the juice from the melon mixture over the salad. Drizzle with additional olive oil and some flaky salt.

perfect little Strawberries

Mr. Arlo at the Watchman's Cabin

Sunset at Bernie & Christy's in Edison Wa.

Oven-Dried Tomatoes with Whipped Feta, Mint, and Basil

Serves 4

When you are working on an outdoor meal, it is great to have some snacks that you can plonk together without thinking, so that you can focus on the fire, or the corn shucking, or the sunset. This is such a delicious treat, simple as it is.

16 Oven-Dried Tomatoes (page 29), sliced into strips (from 8 tomatoes)

¼ cup (60 ml) olive oil, plus more for drizzling

2 teaspoons red wine vinegar

¼ cup (13 g) mint leaves, torn, some whole leaves reserved

⅓ cup (15 g) basil leaves, torn, some whole leaves reserved

1½ cups (360 ml) Whipped Feta (page 34)

6 slices good sourdough bread, toasted and cut in half on a bias

Flaky salt, to serve

In a small bowl, toss together the dried tomatoes, olive oil, vinegar, and torn mint and basil leaves.

Generously spread the whipped feta onto the toast pieces and arrange on a serving plate. Top each toast with a pile of the tomato mixture. Garnish the toasts with a nice drizzle of olive oil, pinches of flaky salt, and the whole herb leaves.

Work in Progress: Compositions on Sourdough

When you think about artist's media, it's often the paints or pastels that are being talked about, but the surface you choose to work on also makes a difference. As you might be able to tell from this book, sourdough toast is one of my favorite surfaces—it brings a beautiful flavor and texture and helps frame any smaller composition of flavors. Keep details in mind when crafting a toast—take the time to toast it slowly, consider rubbing it with a little bit of garlic before crafting your crostino, and ask yourself if it needs a rivulet of fancy olive oil before serving (usually the answer is yes!).

Grilled Oysters with Garlic Scapes, Anchovies, and Parsley

Serves 4 to 6

Grilling oysters is an occasion in itself. You gather your oysters and gather your friends and get to work shucking before setting the opened oysters over the fire. Here's a place where compound butter really shines: A kiss of rich and feisty flavoring melds with the oysters as they cook over the open flames and helps them become burnished and bubbly in the heat. I use the garlic scape and parsley butter here to deliver a green spark to the oysters, but in general, compound butters (page 62) offer a wonderful chance to experiment with flavors. In other moments, I'll incorporate other herbs, citrus, or chiles into the buttery matrix.

2 dozen oysters in their shells, ideally 2 to 3 inches (5 to 7.5 cm) long

1 batch Garlic Scape, Anchovy, and Parsley Butter (page 64)

Prepare a charcoal grill for medium-high heat: Ideally the coals will still be glowing red but not flaming anymore and the interior temperature is about 425°F (220°C). Brush the grates clean.

Line a couple of sheet pans with paper towels. Shuck each oyster and reserve the top shells. In each oyster, cut the adductor muscle from the bottom shell so it is easier to eat when cooked, but leave the oyster meat and liquor in place. Set each shucked oyster on one of the prepared pans and work to preserve as much liquor as possible in each oyster; you can use the reserved top shells as props if the oysters are inclined to tip over.

Spoon about 1½ teaspoons of the garlic scape butter on each oyster. Place the oysters on the grill and cook until the butter fully melts and the oysters start to firm up to the touch. I like to see the mantle (frilly end of the oyster) start to curl up a bit, and the butter will start to brown and caramelize a bit. Cooking time for a medium oyster is 8 to 10 minutes. Be careful, as some oysters might pop a shell out at you as they cook.

Remove the cooked oysters to a serving plate and eat them quickly. Be careful—they will be hot! But so delicious.

Butternut Squash Soup with Tomato, Garam Masala, and Coconut Cream

Serves 6 to 8

Butternut squash is one of those ingredients that I like but also want to manipulate a bit—all that sweetness needs a bit of punctuation. Here the tomato adds an acidic tartness to balance out the roundness of the roasted squash, while the coconut cream and spice blend add lingering complexity. The soup's a great portable meal too: Poured piping hot out of a thermos, this soup would be a hero on a wintry walk or cross-country ski excursion. This velvety, warm, golden puree really doesn't need more than some crusty bread for dipping. I'm happy to serve it simply, though I also love it with some good toast, topped with shredded clothbound cheddar and broiled until melty.

1 large or 2 small butternut squash (about 3 pounds/1.4 kg)

3 tablespoons olive oil

2 teaspoons salt, plus more as needed

1 yellow onion, roughly chopped

2 cloves garlic, roughly chopped

2-inch (5 cm) piece fresh ginger, peeled and grated

2 teaspoons garam masala

2 medium tomatoes, roughly chopped

½ cup (120 ml) unsweetened coconut cream

1 lime (optional)

Preheat the oven to 350°F (175°C).

Cut the squash in half and remove the seeds. Rub it down with 2 tablespoons of the olive oil and season with 1 teaspoon of the salt. Place on a sheet pan and roast cut-side up for 40 minutes, or until knife tender. Set aside to cool.

Meanwhile, in a large soup pot, heat the remaining 1 tablespoon olive oil over medium heat and sweat the onion until tender, about 5 minutes. Then add the garlic, ginger, and the remaining 1 teaspoon salt. Cook for another 3 minutes. Add the garam masala and cook for another 2 minutes. Stir in the tomatoes.

When the squash is cool enough to handle, scoop out the flesh and add to the pot with the tomatoes and onions. Cover with 6 cups (1.4 liters) water. Increase the heat to medium-high, bring to a soft boil, then lower the heat back down to medium and cook uncovered until the liquid reduces by one-third. Add the coconut cream and, using an immersion blender (or working carefully in batches with a regular blender), puree the soup until very smooth. Check the seasoning and adjust with additional salt or a squeeze of lime if it needs a bit of acidity.

Grilled Pork Ribs with Garlic, Aleppo Pepper, Honey, and Rosemary

Serves 6

When American cooks think "ribs," they often think of cooking them low and slow on the barbecue or braised in the oven. I learned a different approach in Italy that I like too—cooking them over a steady medium-high charcoal fire and religiously flipping and basting them every few minutes for about half an hour. They emerge beautifully caramelized and succulently chewy-tender. I compare it to eating the meaty bone of a pork chop. If you like that, you will love this recipe. I really think a stripped-down recipe like this one demands a charcoal (not gas) fire—it's about the elemental interaction of the flame and the rosemary and the sizzling juices that is hard to reproduce with gas (not to mention the lingering petrol flavor it brings to foods).

4 pounds (1.8 kg) pork spareribs

½ cup (120 ml) plus 1 tablespoon olive oil, plus more to rub on the ribs

1 tablespoon salt

Lots of freshly ground black pepper

2 cloves garlic, thinly sliced

1 tablespoon Aleppo pepper

1 rosemary sprig, extra-long so it sticks up out of the pot as a handle

2 tablespoons honey

About an hour before cooking, pull the ribs out of the refrigerator. Season the ribs with 1 tablespoon of the olive oil, rubbing it all over with your hands. Sprinkle with the salt and pepper.

Prepare your grill 30 to 40 minutes before you want to start cooking.

In a small saucepan with a heatproof handle, combine the remaining ½ cup (120 ml) olive oil, the garlic, and Aleppo pepper. Stir to combine using the rosemary sprig.

Once the coals are gray with bright red at their centers, spread them to make a medium-high heat and let the grate heat up for 5 minutes. While it is heating, brush it off and oil it using a pair of tongs and a paper towel drizzled with a bit of oil. Lay the rib rack on the grill. Place the saucepan on the grate nearby, with the rosemary stuck in it, stick-side up. Cook the ribs for 4 minutes. Brush the ribs with the olive oil using the rosemary sprig. Continue cooking for a total of 30 minutes, basting and flipping every 4 minutes. If the barbecue flares up, remove the ribs for a moment to avoid burning them, then reposition them over

(Recipe continues)

a less active part of the coals. If the garlic starts to brown, remove the oil and herb mixture from the grill.

After 30 minutes, check the ribs for doneness: A paring knife stuck into the meat should enter without resistance. Check the meat in several points. If the meat is ready, stir the honey into the hot oil for it to melt and combine flavors. Brush the ribs with the mixture on both sides and cook for about 90 seconds on each side, letting the ribs brown but not blacken. Remove the racks and let them rest for 10 minutes before carving the ribs apart. Place the ribs on a platter and brush one last time with the olive oil–honey mixture. Serve right away. No silver needed! Use your hands—it will taste better.

Work in Progress: Audience Participation

I love serving messy food that my guests have to put a little work into eating—these ribs, or crabs and spot prawns in their shells, steamed artichokes, or grilled young fava beans still in their pods. Don't underestimate the creative entertainment value of making your guests be active at the table—it's a way to kick off conversation and laughter. And I think it gives everyone a greater appreciation of the natural form of those ingredients.

Hama Hama Oyster Co. Lilliwaup, WA

Me and Mr. Arlo

Our backyard!

Green Chermoula Chicken with Yogurt and Radishes

Serves 6 to 8

My Moroccan friend Mehdi first introduced me to chermoula as a marinade for seafood, but I love it on chicken too. It wraps the meat with the soft distinct flavor of cooked cilantro and the gentle warmth of sweet paprika. This is a great picnicky recipe to double up for a summertime crowd, since chicken thighs (or hindquarters) are very forgiving for the busy home cook. I like to use my wood-burning pizza oven outdoors, but an indoor oven works just fine.

2 bunches cilantro leaves (about 2 cups/120 g)

1 bunch parsley leaves (about 1½ cups/90 g)

4 cloves garlic, peeled

1½ teaspoons salt

1 teaspoon sweet paprika

¼ teaspoon cayenne pepper

1 tablespoon cumin seeds, toasted and ground

1 tablespoon coriander seeds, toasted and ground

Juice of 1 large lemon (about ¼ cup/60 ml)

1½ cups (360 ml) olive oil, plus more to drizzle

4 chicken hindquarters or 8 thighs (about 2 pounds/910 g)

½ cup (120 ml) plain whole milk (not Greek) yogurt, to finish

Baby radishes or shaved radishes, to garnish

Preheat the oven (indoor or outdoor!) to 450°F (230°C).

Finely chop the cilantro, parsley, and garlic and put them in a bowl. Add the salt, paprika, cayenne, cumin, and coriander. Add the lemon juice and give it a stir, then add the olive oil.

Using half of the chermoula, rub each piece of chicken with it (on both sides) and set aside. When ready to cook, place skin-side up on a sheet pan, put it in the oven, and roast 25 to 30 minutes, with the hindquarters taking a bit longer. You can use an instant-read thermometer to double-check their doneness (165°F/74°C) before pulling from the oven. Pile the chicken on a serving platter and drizzle with yogurt and olive oil and garnish with radishes.

The remaining chermoula can be stored in the fridge for a day or two and tossed with warm cooked potatoes or spooned into a bowl of steamed mussels or clams.

Hama Hama Clams at the Watchman's Cabin with Stinging Nettle Butter, Crème Fraîche, and Preserved Lemon

Serves 4 to 6

The Watchman's Cabin is a sweet little A-frame house built by Adam James, famed oyster farmer, right on the beach at Hama Hama on the Hood Canal in Washington. It's where I fell in love with my husband, Dan, who was working at Hama Hama Oyster Company at the time. The cabin is a place that has become a second home to us.

At the cabin, we can sit on the deck and hear the sea lions talk to each other, watch the sea smoke roll in, and breathe in the beauty of this wild gorgeous spot. I have cooked more pots of clams in this cabin and on this beach than I have anywhere else.

There's nothing like eating shellfish at the waterfront: The salt air almost works to season the meal. If you're extra outdoorsy, you could cook these scrumptious clams—seasoned with dark green nettle butter—on a grill or in a campfire. But otherwise, just carry them out from the kitchen while they are piping hot and serve with crackle-crusted baguettes and a cold, aromatic white wine (like Muscadet). Don't forget a bowl for the empty shells, which you can toss in the water when you're done (if you are seaside).

2 cups (480 ml) dry white vermouth (Dolin is a good option)

2 pounds (910 g) Manila or other small clams, cleaned

1 cup (230 g) Stinging Nettle Butter (recipe follows)

Peel from 1 preserved lemon, sliced into long, thin strips, pith and flesh removed (you can use the rest in a braised beef dish)

Salt and freshly ground black pepper

Juice of 1 lemon

1 cup (240 ml) crème fraîche

Crusty bread, to serve

In a large pot with a lid, warm the vermouth over medium-high heat. When it comes to a simmer, add the clams, cover, and steam until most of the clams are open, about 4 minutes. Reduce the heat to medium, add the nettle butter and preserved lemon strips, and stir. Re-cover and cook for 2 more minutes, or until the butter is melted. If at that point there are unopened clams, remove and discard them.

Check the seasoning, adding salt, pepper, and/or a squeeze of lemon juice to taste. Serve in large low bowls with a dollop of crème fraîche and some of your favorite bread to dip in the broth.

Stinging Nettle Butter

Makes 2½ cups (568 g)

If it's spring in the Pacific Northwest, that means STINGING NETTLES! These delicious and nutritious greens are popping up all over the place, in parks, alongside the road, and thankfully in the local farmers' market. The forest greens actually sting, so until they are cooked you need to wear gloves. I use garden gloves. Be careful! Have fun! Use any leftover nettle butter in another pot of clams or as a wonderful addition to risotto.

8 ounces (225 g) stinging nettles (snip away and discard any tough stems with scissors; the little ones are OK)

3 tablespoons olive oil

2 cloves garlic, roughly chopped

1 shallot, minced

1 teaspoon salt, plus more as needed

1 cup (2 sticks/225 g) unsalted butter, cut into cubes, at room temperature

Freshly ground black pepper

Bring a large pot of water to a boil. Have ready a big bowl filled with ice water. Dunk the nettles into the boiling water, making sure they are submerged. Simmer for 3 minutes, or until they turn bright dark green.

Strain the nettles from the liquid and plunge them in the ice water. Don't throw the cooking liquid away—it is amazing as tea or as a stock for risotto.

Warm the olive oil in a medium saucepan over medium heat, then add the garlic, shallot, and salt. Cook, stirring occasionally, until tender and translucent, about 4 minutes. Meanwhile, grab a handful of the (cooked! cooled!) nettles and squeeze out any excess water and continue with the rest of the nettles. Coarsely chop the nettles, then add to the sweated shallots and garlic and cook for another 2 minutes. Let cool to room temperature.

Transfer the nettle mixture to a food processor and buzz for a minute, then add the butter one cube at a time. Keep it running for another 2 to 3 minutes, until it comes together into an emulsion. It will change in color and get a bit lighter and very bright green. Taste the mixture and season with additional salt and black pepper as desired.

Wrap tightly and store the stinging nettle butter in the fridge for up to 2 weeks. You can also freeze it for a couple of months.

A Couple of Offbeat Steaks with Lemon, Anchovy, and Caper Butter

Serves 6 to 8

Here's a fun experiment: Try out a couple of different cuts next time you have the grill lit. There's no better way to learn about cuts than to do a mixed grill and taste them side by side. My experience owning a whole-animal steak restaurant has given me a much broader appreciation of less "steaky" steaks and it has given me the pleasure to help our guests discover underappreciated cuts like chuck eye, velvet, and ranch steaks. This recipe demonstrates two favorites of mine that aren't too tricky to source: top sirloin and hanger steak, or onglet.

The top sirloin is denser, and the hanger steak has a loose structure and a wonderful meaty flavor. The simple steaks go wonderfully with my easy go-to lemon, anchovy, and caper butter, which I keep stashed in the freezer.

Note: If you can't grill where you are, you can sear the steaks in a cast-iron skillet; just make sure to preheat it thoroughly.

2 (16- to 18-ounce/454 to 510 g) hanger steaks

1 (16- to 18-ounce/454 to 510 g) top sirloin steak, about 1½ inches (4 cm) thick

Salt

Freshly ground black pepper

Olive oil, for cooking

½ batch Lemon, Anchovy, and Caper Compound Butter (page 62), softened

Flaky salt, to serve

Season the steaks generously with salt and pepper. Let them sit out of the refrigerator while you prepare the grill, about 30 minutes before cooking. When the charcoal is glowing but ashed over, spread the coals, leaving a good hot pile on one side. Place the grate on top and let it heat up.

Rub the steaks with a bit of olive oil and place them on the hot part of the grate. Cook the hanger steaks for 4 minutes on each side. The top sirloin takes a bit longer, 5 to 6 minutes per side. If you want to measure them with a thermometer, pull the meat at 125°F (52°C) for medium-rare. Remove the meat from the grill to a platter and liberally baste it with the compound butter. Let it sit for at least 10 minutes before slicing.

When ready to serve, warm the remaining compound butter to melt it. Cut each hanger steak in plump slices across the grain on the diagonal. Slice the top sirloin more thinly. Lay out on a serving plate and spoon the butter over the slices. Sprinkle the meat with flaky salt and serve any extra compound butter in a bowl alongside.

Sunday Dinners

The Joy of Leisurely Cooking

Over the years, it's been a goal of mine to take the stuffiness out of restaurant dining, and I look for the same ease when I have people over for a meal. Of course, I love to cook for birthdays and holidays, but I have grown to particularly appreciate the pleasures of having people over for no special occasion at all. Time is so scarce in everyday life, which is why I love the idea of Sunday dinners, held not for obligation but simply to appreciate the people in my life. Each one is a small ritual way to reclaim time, stretch it to my liking, and remind me that busyness does not equal happiness.

Sunday dinners don't really need to take place on Sundays. With my crazy schedule, it's not infrequent that I move the supper to another day when I am available and able to spend more time cooking. So, Sunday is less a day than a mode of cooking and eating. Cooking for a tableful of friends or family takes time, and I like to enjoy it. The food I make is always very seasonal: long, lazy grilling sessions in the summer or delicious things braised in Dutch ovens in the fall and winter. Sunday cooking mode isn't meant to be the most intricate food I can make—it means stripping back complications and cooking slowly— the kind of food that can handle developing in the background while I putter around with other tasks too. These meals have a pre-modern feeling: They could adapt to being cooked in a fireplace if a November gale suddenly put out the power.

The food I serve at Sunday dinners tends to be a little, well, brown or beige. I'm drawn to intensely flavored, sometimes stewy food—braised beef shins, beans with sausage, oyster stew. Brown food may not be the flashiest to photograph, but it has layers of flavor and a deeply restorative quality.

An adage suggests that you don't try cooking a dish for the first time with guests coming over, but I do it all the time. I say if you have the correct sort of guests on their way—like maybe not your intimidating boss or your super-critical mother-in-law—you should go ahead and try something new for them. Don't pretend you know exactly what you're doing: Let them in on your process. "Let's try this and see what

happens!" is a fairly fun and inviting way to start an evening together. If you are working with nice ingredients and not too far from your technical comfort zone, then likely as not, you'll make something delicious. Your friends can help you think how you might tweak it into a regular part of your repertoire. And even if it's not a thrilling result, how terrible is that? You can raid your pantry to cook up some spaghetti and still have a fun time at the table. It's the company that matters most, and why not share the creative process with them?

The one difference I make with hosting people for dinner is serving multiple courses instead of just one. Honestly, even that is kind of a cheat, though, as I count a snack before dinner as a course! I'm never quite ready when guests come over, so having a hearty smoked fish dip or a pretty cheese plate at the ready helps everyone feel good while I continue to get my act together. I know I can still feed people and have them happy to be in the midst of things as I unpack the last few groceries that I ran out to get or I chat to my dog Arlo about how the braised beef is progressing. I feel like I would never have people over if everything had to be just right.

When I plan a dinner, I almost always start by writing a menu out longhand and taping it to the tile by the stove. A menu helps rev me up for the meal and get excited about the creative project ahead. It's also a little prompt to keep me focused, even if I get pulled away for a bit, but I don't take it too seriously; I'll revise and adjust along the way. Sunday-style dinners are often cooked a day or two ahead: Most braises, gratins, and soups improve with a short sojourn in the fridge. The major work is then achieved by the time friends arrive. This allows time for the other aspects of Sunday dining: the details that make a meal a happy ritual—getting the fireplace ready to light with a few rosemary sprigs amid the wood to scent the house, choosing the playlist (or spinning a record), snipping a few flowers or conifer branches to put in the vase. I'll chat with Dan about choosing the wine so we can open any red that could use a breather. Often my coziest dinners are fall or winter affairs, when the sky gets dark before 4 p.m. I've learned to treat candles as essential mood-boosters in the darkest months here in Seattle, and often choose to go a little overboard with them. I don't want anything to feel fussy, but I do like to build a casual sense of ceremony because I value my time around the table with people I love. I have lived in my little bungalow and have made a point of cooking for friends and family there since the early 2000s. It's not one of those grand houses set up for entertaining with a walk-in pantry and a high-ceilinged dining room, so coziness is mandatory. And, frankly, that's the way I like it.

My hope with a Sunday meal is to stretch out that time together. If it's possible I'd rather not have friends show up and get eating within a half hour. If there is time, I love a long afternoon of sipping and chatting and maybe painting or picking herbs or shelling beans. Once we do sit, I'm inclined to have the meal served family style, passed hand to hand around the table. I look forward to a stretched-out meal, filled with shared memories, upcoming plans, plenty of laughter, and maybe a little bit of gossip. Though I don't necessarily plan for dessert on an ordinary weeknight, I almost always serve dessert at a Sunday dinner to deepen the sense of delight and to keep people around the table. And then maybe a bit of tea, or coffee, or Armagnac. I'll clear the table but not get started on the dishes in earnest while folks are over; I don't want to suggest that people should get home soon. There's one more way I like to shape time with my Sunday suppers: The next day, when the dishes are put away and the tablecloth is in the wash, I like to copy that original menu into a notebook—it's a record of the food I made, and helpful for cookbooks like this one! But it's also a way to pin down that moment in my memory. That moment of reflection keeps the evening from fluttering off into the forgotten past.

Smoked Salmon Rillettes with Piment d'Espelette, Dill, and Toast

Serves 6 to 8

I love a smoked fish dip—or spread—as this one is more properly categorized. Not only is it a delicious starter, but it's truly easy to make (and even make a day ahead if you want—just wait to add the dill until right before serving), so you have something ready when people arrive and you're still finishing dinner. The gentle heat from the Basque red pepper and a shower of fresh dill make this extra special. But keep in mind that it should be rustic too—don't make the mixture too smooth in the food processor, and don't try to smooth out the top of the dip. Let it be bumpy, and serve it with really good toast.

5 to 6 ounces (140 to 170 g) hot-smoked (kippered) wild sockeye salmon, skin removed (and saved for your dog's next dinner, just make sure there are no bones)

8 ounces (225 g) cream cheese

½ teaspoon piment d'Espelette

Grated zest of 1 small lemon

2 tablespoons lemon juice

1 teaspoon salt

¼ cup (60 ml) olive oil, plus more to serve

3 ounces (85 g) cold-smoked wild sockeye salmon, skin removed, if needed (your dog's next dinner—just make sure there are no bones)

¼ cup (9 g) dill, lightly chopped, plus some whole sprigs, for garnish

Cornichons, to serve

Toasted rye bread or baguette, to serve

In a food processor, pulse the hot-smoked salmon with the cream cheese, piment d'Espelette, lemon zest and juice, salt, and ¼ cup olive oil. This mixture breaks down quickly, so don't overprocess. With a rubber spatula, transfer the salmon mixture to a medium bowl. Mince the cold-smoked-style salmon and fold that into the cream cheese mixture, then fold in the dill. Check for seasoning and move to your desired serving bowl, but do not flatten it—you want some bumps and crags on the surface. Put in the fridge to firm up for at least 1 hour. If refrigerated longer or overnight, cover with plastic wrap. Drizzle with olive oil, garnish with the sprigs of dill, and serve with a pot of cornichons and toasted rye or baguette.

Poached Chicken with Fennel, Daikon, and Horseradish Crème Fraîche

Serves 4

The inspiration for this dish is pot au feu, the classic French simmered meat and vegetable dish, usually made with beef, but this a lovely way to prepare a whole chicken too. As much as I adore roast chicken, there is also an irreplaceable velvet quality to poached chicken meat, and the wonderful bonus of a rich cooking broth to serve as soup and sauce at once. And there's no better way to prep meat for chicken salad.

While poached chicken is an old favorite, I always strive to learn new techniques. Thanks to Anna Tobias, the London chef and owner of Café Deco, I picked up a new way to prepare it. This cooking method seems a little scary at first: You bring your chicken to a boil in a flavorful liquid, then cover the pot and turn off the heat, letting the chicken cook in the residual heat. The reason? It's very easy to (paradoxically) dry chicken out when you cook it in liquid, and this method makes sure that you don't end up with a stringy, sad bird. For this variation on her technique, I provide two condiments: Try both, or just make one if your time is limited!

(Recipe continues)

For the chicken:

10 sprigs thyme

2 bay leaves, fresh, if possible

6 sprigs parsley

1 (3 to 3½-pound/1.4 to 1.6 kg) chicken

2 tablespoons salt, plus more as needed

1 teaspoon black peppercorns

2 stalks celery, diagonally sliced into 1-inch (2.5 cm) pieces

2 jalapeño chiles, halved and seeded

1 (4-inch/10 cm) piece fresh ginger, halved lengthwise

6 to 8 small Yukon Gold potatoes, peeled and halved

2 fennel bulbs, cut into 4 to 6 wedges (depending on the size of the fennel)

Thinly slivered purple daikon slices (optional)

Flaky salt, to serve

1 batch Jalapeño Green Sauce (page 25)

For the Horseradish Crème Fraîche:

1 cup (240 ml) crème fraîche

1 tablespoon olive oil

2 inches (5 cm) fresh horseradish, peeled and grated

½ teaspoon salt, plus more as needed

Freshly ground black pepper

To make the chicken: Gather the thyme, bay leaves, and parsley together in a bouquet and tie together with kitchen twine. Season the chicken with the fine sea salt.

Place the chicken in a large, heavy stockpot or Dutch oven (you want to make sure the pot is spacious enough: There needs to be a few inches of space around and above the chicken in order for it to cook properly—mine is 7¼ quarts (6.9 liters), 5 inches (12 cm) tall, and 11 inches (28 cm) across. Add 11 cups (2.6 liters) water, the bouquet of herbs, peppercorns, celery, chiles, and ginger. Bring to a boil over high heat. Put a lid on it and turn off the heat. Let the chicken rest in the pot and don't open the lid for 1 hour and 40 minutes.

Pull out the chicken and cover it in foil.

Strain the cooking liquid, clean the pot, and return the liquid to it. Add the potatoes and bring to a boil over high heat. Turn the heat down to maintain a gentle simmer and cook for 10 minutes. Add the fennel wedges and cook until both the potatoes and fennel are tender, 5 to 10 minutes. Taste the broth and adjust the seasoning with fine sea salt.

While the vegetables are cooking, make the horse-radish sauce: In a small bowl, stir together the crème fraîche, olive oil, horseradish, and salt. Taste and season with more salt, if needed, and pepper. Be generous with the pepper in this sauce!

Pull the meat into chunky pieces and lay in a deep serving dish.

When the vegetables are tender, distribute the potatoes and fennel around the meat. Ladle hot broth into the serving dish. Sprinkle with daikon slices, if using, and flaky salt. Serve the chicken with the green sauce and horseradish crème fraîche on the side.

White Beans with Pork Sausage, Lemon Peel, and Green Herbs

Serves 4 to 6

Sausage and beans couldn't be a simpler meal, but it's such a satisfying classic. Here's the part that really makes this version special: a careless abundance of herbs and, yes, a little bit of crème fraîche too. When in doubt, throw in herbs, lots of them. That's very much my motto, and you'll see why when you taste how vibrant these beans are. The other secret to a simple dish like this is high-quality beans like those from Rancho Gordo. I never buy too many at a time because I want to make sure my dried beans are as fresh as possible (and because I only have so much space in my little Seattle kitchen). Fresher beans also cook faster than ancient ones.

4 cups (960 ml) chicken stock

4 tablespoons (60 ml) olive oil, plus more to drizzle

½ yellow onion, root intact to keep from falling apart

4 cloves garlic, thinly sliced

Zest of 1 lemon, julienned

1 bay leaf

Pinch of red chile flakes

2 cups (370 g) dried white beans (like Purgatorio or cannellini), soaked overnight, drained (see Note)

1 teaspoon fine sea salt, plus more as needed

1 cup (60 g) loosely packed mint leaves, picked and loosely chopped, plus a few whole leaves to garnish

1 cup (240 ml) crème fraîche

1 cup (60 g) dill, picked and loosely chopped, plus a few whole fronds to garnish

(Ingredients continue)

Warm the chicken stock in a medium saucepan over medium heat.

In a large, heavy saucepan or Dutch oven, heat 2 tablespoons of the olive oil over medium heat. Add the onion, garlic, lemon peel, bay leaf, and chile flakes and cook until the garlic is fragrant, about 1 minute.

Add the beans and stir well to coat with the oil. Ladle in about 2 cups (480 ml) of the chicken stock and stir in the fine sea salt. Let the mixture come to a boil, then turn down the heat to maintain a lively simmer. Ladle in more chicken stock as necessary to make sure the beans are immersed. Cook until the beans are tender but not falling apart. This can vary with the variety and freshness of the beans, but start checking around 25 minutes in (they may take as long as 45 minutes). When they are done, remove from the heat and pull out the onion and bay leaf, but leave the beans in their liquid.

To cook the sausage, heat a heavy steel skillet over medium-high heat. Add the remaining 2 tablespoons olive oil. When the oil shimmers, add the sausages. Poke a few holes in each sausage with a sharp tip of a paring knife. Brown the sausages on each side, about 4 minutes per side. Continue cooking until the sausage juices run clear, perhaps a minute more.

(Recipe continues)

1 cup (60 g) tarragon leaves, picked and loosely chopped, plus a few whole leaves to garnish

About 1 pound (455 g) fresh pork sausages, Italian or French style (not a sweet breakfast sausage)

Freshly ground black pepper

Lemon juice (optional)

Flaky salt

When ready to serve, remove 1½ cups (360 ml) of the bean-cooking liquid (you can use this for a soup base later!). Warm the beans up over medium heat, then stir in the crème fraîche and all the chopped herbs. Season with fine sea salt, black pepper, and a bit of lemon juice, if needed. Place the beans and their juices in a serving dish. Top with the warm grilled sausages. Garnish with the whole dill, tarragon, and mint leaves. Finish with a sprinkling of flaky salt and a bit of olive oil.

Note: If you forgot to soak your beans, here are two tips to hurry things along: 1) use the freshest beans you can—high-quality, more recently dried beans cook quicker; 2) cover the beans with boiling water, leave for an hour, then drain and cook—that will get you to a point that's close to an overnight soak.

Work in Progress: Viridian Greens

Using fresh herbs is among my trustiest ways to tune a dish—their freshness, bright flavor, and just plain greenness all help me find a connection to straightforward preparations. Keep in mind as you play with them that each form of herb brings a little something different to the dish. Whole leaves and fronds add loft and a natural vibe to a plate. Finely chopped herbs get into more places and permeate more flavor than rougher chops. Fried herbs give crackle and crunch as a final topping. And pestos and green sauces can add a swish and a swirl of visual interest to a plate that's looking stiff and blocky.

Looking out towards the Columbia River, Wa

Dreamy Mr. Arlo

Crab painting in my sketchbook

Charred Squid with Pan-Roasted Fennel, Ginger, and Lime

Serves 2 to 4

I'm always looking for seafood that is more sustainable than the average. Squid are so low on the ocean food chain that you can eat them with less concern than many finfish. They grow fast, reproduce abundantly, and die within a year. I'm a big fryer of calamari, but I have recently been sautéing it more as a main course: It's so quick and easy that it has become a midweek favorite with a side of steamed rice. In this version, the roasted fennel has a loopy, tentacle-like shape to echo the squid, and a gingery lime fish sauce pays homage to the incredible Vietnamese restaurants here in Seattle. If you like a little heat, do serve this with chili crisp: I love KariKari, made right here in the Pacific Northwest.

2-inch (5 cm) piece fresh ginger, peeled and finely grated

2 cloves garlic, minced

Zest and juice of 1 lime

About ½ cup (20 g) minced fresh cilantro leaves, plus another dozen sprigs to garnish

Pinch of red chile flakes

1 small serrano chile, seeded and minced

2 tablespoons fish sauce (I like Red Boat), plus more for serving

½ teaspoon sugar

1 pound (455 g) squid, defrosted and cleaned (see Note)

2 medium fennel bulbs, each cut lengthwise into ½-inch (12 mm) slices

2 tablespoons plus 2 teaspoons canola oil

Salt

(Ingredients continue)

In a small bowl, combine the ginger, garlic, lime zest and juice, cilantro, chile flakes, chile, fish sauce, and sugar. Set aside.

Rinse the squid, then slice it into rounds, 3 to 4 per tube. Set on a paper towel to dry off. Drying is important so you can get a nice sear on the squid.

Set up a simple steamer with an inch of water in the bottom of the pot. Bring the water to a boil and place the fennel in a basket in a thin even layer. Cover the lid once you see steam coming up from below, turn the heat to medium-high and cook for about 5 minutes, until the fennel is barely soft when poked with a pointy knife. Drain and pat dry.

Heat 2 teaspoons of the canola oil in a large, heavy skillet over medium-high heat. Gently lay the steamed fennel into the pan in a single layer; you will need to work in batches. Cook each side for about 2 minutes, until golden brown. Season lightly with salt and set aside.

In an even larger skillet (about 12 inches/30 cm) if you have one, heat the remaining 2 tablespoons canola oil over high heat until shimmering. Working in 3 batches, add a third of the squid and cook for about 5 minutes, turning once only. Season with a touch of salt. You will

(Recipe continues)

Lime wedges, to serve

Olive oil

Steamed brown rice, to serve

Chili crisp condiment, to serve
(optional)

notice a distinct and delicious minerally smell—
essentially a briny char with crisp caramelized edges.

Toss the hot squid with a spoonful of ginger sauce,
then remove the squid and juices to a serving dish.
Wipe out the pan and repeat the cooking process
for the remaining two batches of squid, tossing the
newly cooked squid with another spoonful of sauce
each time. After the last batch, return all the squid to
the pan and toss well.

When all the squid is mixed, mix in the roasted fennel
and taste the seasoning, adjusting with juice from a
lime wedge or salt to taste. Place the squid and its
juices in a serving dish, drape with cilantro sprigs,
and place lime wedges around the plate. Drizzle with
a little olive oil and serve with rice, additional fish
sauce, and chili crisp, if using, on the side.

Note: Go ahead and buy frozen squid! Fresh squid is
lovely but messy and time-consuming to process. I
buy frozen squid and let it defrost in the refrigerator
overnight. I rinse it quickly before cooking to whisk
away any little hard bits of cartilage that may have
stuck to the ice. I cut the hoods into ½-inch (12 mm)
tubes and generally keep the tentacles whole. Once
rinsed, I lay them out on paper towels to dry before
cooking: that helps them crisp up rather than steam
in the pan.

Grand Aioli with Smoked Black Cod, Mussels, and Summer Vegetables

Serves 4 to 6

When I go to a summertime farmers' market, I tend to get a little greedy, bringing home all the tender new beans and plump tomatoes and baby beets with their topknots of shiny leaves. This Northwest take on the Provençal classic grand aioli is the dish for when I have done just that. It's a gorgeous great big platter of seafood and summer vegetables, some cooked, some raw. And of course, the aioli, an irresistible bowl of garlic-scented mayonnaise to dip everything in. We get hot-smoked black cod here in Seattle easily at our farmers' markets and good groceries. On the East Coast, the same fish might be called kippered sable. In any case, you can find smoked black cod from Pike Place Fish Market (which ships all sorts of specialty foods around the country—it's a wonderful resource). And please shift this meal for your season and your market: It's ripe for adaptation to the radishes and snap peas of spring or the full spectrum of chicories and carrots in the fall.

Salt

1 pound (455 g) green beans

8 baby beets, root end and a few small leaves attached

1 teaspoon olive oil, plus more to drizzle

1 clove garlic, thinly sliced

Pinch of red chile flakes

2 pounds (910 g) mussels, cleaned well and stringy beards removed

½ cup (120 ml) white wine

Lemon juice, as needed

1 batch aioli (page 46)

1½ pounds (680 g) smoked black cod, broken into morsels

(Ingredients continue)

Have ready a large bowl of ice water. Fill a large pot with water and salt it heavily. Bring to a boil over high heat and add the green beans. Cook the beans until they are crisp-tender, 2 to 3 minutes after the water boils again, then lift them out of the pot and immediately place them in the ice water to stop the cooking. When cool, remove the beans from the ice water onto a plate lined with a clean kitchen towel. Turn the heat back to high and bring the water back to a boil. Add the beets, turn the heat down to maintain a simmer, and cook until the beets are mostly tender but still firm at the center when poked with a small knife, 10 to 15 minutes. Remove the beets from the water and let cool to room temperature. Slice the beets in half.

Heat a small, lidded pot that holds the mussels in a shallow layer over medium heat. Add the olive oil, garlic, and chile flakes and cook for 30 seconds, or until fragrant. Add the mussels and wine, cover with the lid, and cook until the mussels steam themselves open. Remove the open mussels, then cook a bit more to see if more will open. Discard any mussels

(Recipe continues)

1 large fennel bulb, sliced lengthwise into slices about ¼ inch (6 mm) thick

1½ pints (430 g) cherry tomatoes

3 small farmers' market slicing cucumbers, sharply sliced on the bias

2 heads small crunchy lettuces, like little gems, or 2 heads Belgian endive leaves, separated

1 baguette, sliced thick and grilled or toasted, to serve

that refuse to open after 4 to 5 minutes. When cool enough to handle, remove the cooked mussels from their shells, drizzle with olive oil and a squeeze of lemon, and keep in the fridge, covered, until you are ready to serve them.

To assemble, find the biggest platter you can. Arrange the cod pieces in a low bowl and lay the mussels on top of them (just the mussels, not their liquid). Drizzle them well with olive oil. Place the aioli in another small bowl and place it on the platter. Assemble the remaining elements around the two bowls on the platter: the beets, green beans, fennel, tomatoes, cucumbers, and lettuce leaves. Tuck the baguette slices in and around the vegetables. Serve as soon as it is assembled.

If you make it ahead, temper the cod and mussels out of the fridge 15 minutes before serving and keep the remaining elements in the fridge until serving time— they are best cold and crispy.

Work in Progress: The Power of a Platter

Looking at the previous recipe, it might seem like a lot, but, really, it's largely a lot of arranging and not that much cooking. A grand aioli is so fun because with one giant platter—OK, that and a loaf of bread—you can call it a meal. Always keep in mind that a little bit of this and a little bit of that can be a wonderful way to eat with friends. Cheese and charcuterie boards or tinned fish and crudités are ways to celebrate with a group without getting too formal-dinner-party about it.

Braised Duck Legs with Olives, Rosemary, and Garlic

Serves 4

When we think duck legs, we often think confit, which is a classic for a reason. But duck confit takes premeditation: You need to cure the duck legs and find enough duck fat to submerge the legs and then cook everything *veeeery* slowly for hours. Again, totally delicious, and long lasting once cooked, but the kind of dish that you plan for. Braised duck legs, on the other hand, come together with just a bit of labor and a couple of hours in the oven. I like to serve them with a simple lentil salad—cooked French lentils with chopped cucumbers and tomatoes, minced preserved lemon, and tons of basil dressed with olive oil and lemon juice. If you end up with any extra duck, the pulled meat is delicious in pasta or crisped and tossed with frisée salad (see page 113).

4 duck legs (about 2 pounds/910 g), any extra blobby fat trimmed off

Salt and freshly ground black pepper

¼ cup (60 ml) olive oil

1 yellow onion, peeled and cut into 8 wedges

1 head garlic, sliced in half across the middle

2 (4-inch/10 cm) sprigs rosemary

8 to 10 sprigs thyme, tied with kitchen twine

½ teaspoon red chile flakes

2 cups (480 ml) dry white wine

2 cups (480 ml) chicken stock

Zest of 1 lemon, cut into thin slivers

8 ounces (225 g) green olives, like Lucques

The night before cooking, cut the skin on the shin bone of each duck leg just above the knobby ankle bone. Season the duck legs with salt and lots of black pepper. Place on a plate or flat dish, uncovered, and refrigerate overnight.

Preheat the oven to 350°F (175°C).

In a large, heavy skillet that can hold 4 duck legs, heat the olive oil over medium-high heat. When the oil shimmers, add the seasoned duck and sear on both sides until browned, 4 to 5 minutes per side. Remove from the pan and set aside. Pour out all but 2 tablespoons of the fat.

Add the onion, garlic, rosemary, thyme, and chile flakes and sauté for about 2 minutes, until the onions just start to soften and brown. Pour in the wine and chicken stock and scrape up any browned bits left on the bottom of the pot. Add the lemon zest and olives.

Place the duck legs in a large baking dish. Pour in the white wine–onion combination. The liquid should come about two-thirds of the way up the side of the duck; add a little water if there is not quite enough liquid in the pan. Place in the oven uncovered and braise for 90 minutes to 2 hours—if the meat starts looking too dark, cover the dish with a sheet of foil. The duck is done when a small knife slides easily into the thickest part of the leg. Serve directly from the baking dish.

Big Meatball Feast

Serves 10

Big meatballs. Big feast. You can serve these with spaghetti if you'd like, but you don't have to! I will never forget the first time my brother joined me at a trattoria in Venice. His face lit up when the server brought our table a giant platter of meatballs with no pasta—nothing to get in the way of the delicious polpetti. Just gorgeous, slightly spicy meatballs, slow cooked in tomato sauce and then served with a generous pile of perfect Parmesan cheese. Like those Italian meatballs, these, made with a bit of lemon peel and anchovy for added interest, only need a side of crispy bread to make sure none of the sauce goes to waste. I like my meatballs with a little lightness to them, so I add the breadcrumbs just before shaping the meatballs, not earlier—it seems to keep them tender.

Note: This is a big recipe, because I think meatballs are one of the great party foods. I like the idea of a giant meal around a sprawling outdoor table. It would be dreamy on a lawn under an oak tree, with everyone dressed in pale linens and big fluffy dogs lying around. But in my real life, we'd serve the platter of meatballs on our big marble table, with our dog Arlo drooling and me, in jeans, hoping for it to not rain. If you don't have a party to serve these at, then just toss the extra meatballs and sauce in the freezer for two months or more. Having meatballs in the freezer is a power move.

(Recipe continues)

2 pounds (910 g) ground beef

1 pound (455 g) ground pork

2 tablespoons salt, plus more as needed

Freshly ground black pepper

½ cup (18 g) chopped Italian parsley leaves

Zest of 1 lemon, shaved on a Microplane

4 anchovies, minced

2 cups (200 g) grated pecorino Romano cheese, plus more to serve

2 large eggs, lightly beaten

2 cloves garlic, minced

2 cups (120 g) Plain Dried Breadcrumbs (page 26)

48 ounces (6 cups/1.4 liters) tomato sauce or marinara sauce (see Note)

½ cup (120 ml) olive oil, for frying

Parmigiano-Reggiano cheese, to serve

Cooked spaghetti, to serve (optional)

In a large bowl, combine the ground beef, ground pork, salt, pepper to taste, parsley, lemon peel, anchovies, pecorino cheese, eggs, and garlic. Mix thoroughly with your hands, pinching and folding to make sure all the ingredients are well blended. Gently fold in the breadcrumbs and 1½ cups (360 ml) water and mix to combine. Using your hands, form the meat mixture into 2½-inch (6 cm) balls.

In a large saucepan that can hold the sauce and all the meatballs, heat the tomato sauce over medium-low heat. Heat a large skillet over medium-high heat and pour in the olive oil. When the oil shimmers, fry the meatballs in small batches, carefully rolling them around to brown on all sides, 4 to 5 minutes. The meatballs will be tender, so use a small flat metal spatula to carefully turn them. As they are finished, scoop the browned meatballs from the skillet and slide them into the sauce. When all the meatballs are in the sauce, turn the heat up to maintain a gentle simmer and cook for another 30 minutes. Serve the meatballs and sauce with lots of freshly grated pecorino and Parmigiano, with or without spaghetti. Leftovers freeze well (see Note).

Note: You can purchase your favorite jarred sauce, or try this quick tomato sauce based on Marcella Hazan's famous buttered tomato sauce. In a large, nonreactive saucepan, I combine 1 onion, quartered, 4 tablespoons butter, and 2 (24-ounce/690 g) bottles tomato passata. I bring the mixture to a simmer and let it cook for 40 minutes. Before using it, I fish out the onion quarters and season it with salt and add a pinch of sugar if it is too acidic.

Braised Fennel with Bottarga and Parmigiano-Reggiano Broth

Serves 4 to 6

Bottarga, cured mullet roe, is kind of the Parmesan of the sea: You shave it like cheese over a finished dish, and the amber shreds add salt and funky umami taste to whatever they land on. Here I've teamed bottarga up with Parmigiano broth (page 53) to make a very rich tasting fennel braise. It's so juicy and good that it could be the star of a veg-forward dinner, but it also makes a succulent side for grilled lamb (page 226). You'll end up with extra bottarga after this: You can shave it onto scrambled eggs or any number of pasta dishes, or simply make the fennel again. Well-wrapped bottarga lasts for weeks in the refrigerator.

2 tablespoons olive oil

3 tablespoons unsalted butter

2 cloves garlic, peeled

4 medium-large fennel bulbs (about 1 pound/455 g each), cut into 1½-inch (4 cm) wedges, tender inner fronds reserved, if possible

Zest of 1 lemon, slivered

¾ teaspoon red chile flakes, plus a pinch to garnish

2 cups (480 ml) Parmigiano-Reggiano Broth (page 53)

2 tablespoons lemon juice

1-inch (2.5 cm) piece bottarga (about 1 ounce/25 g)

In a large, heavy saucepan over medium heat, warm the olive oil and 2 tablespoons of the butter with the garlic. Cook the garlic for 2 minutes, then remove it. Add half of the fennel wedges, making sure not to crowd the pan. Cook the fennel attentively, browning it on both sides, about 8 minutes total. Set the browned fennel on a plate and cook the remaining fennel.

Return the cooked fennel to the pan and sprinkle in the lemon zest, chile flakes, and fennel fronds, if available. Pour in the Parmigiano broth, increase the heat to high, and bring to a boil. Turn the heat down to maintain a gentle simmer, cover, and cook until the wedges are tender when poked with a knife at their thickest part, about 15 minutes.

Remove the fennel from the liquid and return the pan to the stovetop. Increase the heat to high, bring the liquid to a boil, and cook until reduced by half, about 6 minutes. Add the remaining 1 tablespoon butter and the lemon juice and swirl the pan to melt and emulsify the butter. Pour the liquid over the fennel. Sprinkle a pinch of chile flakes over the fennel, then grate the bottarga all over. Serve immediately.

Grilled Lamb with Aleppo Pepper, Whipped Tahini, and Nectarines

Serves 4 to 6

This recipe is a tribute to summer, and I make it with a variety of quick-cooking lamb cuts. Lamb leg steaks and blade chops are lean, meaty, and inexpensive. The leg steaks are juicy, and the blade chops are a bit like a chicken drumstick—a bit more work to eat around the bones, but worth it for their succulent flavor. Since you can't always be sure what the meat department has in stock, you can always use classic rib chops in their stead. So, use whatever cuts you like, but do your best to find meat from a local farm.

3 cloves garlic, grated

1 teaspoon Aleppo pepper

5 tablespoons (75 ml) olive oil, plus more to serve

2 teaspoons salt

28 to 32 ounces (800 to 910 g) lamb cuts (leg steaks, blade chops, and/or lamb chops), ideally about 1 inch (2.5 cm) thick

4 nectarines, pitted and halved (or if cling-style, cut off the pit in large chunks)

Flaky salt, to serve

1½ cups (360 ml) Whipped Tahini (page 38)

Ginger Green Sauce, to serve (optional; page 25)

In a medium bowl that can hold the meat, whisk together the garlic, Aleppo pepper, ¼ cup (60 ml) of the olive oil, and the salt. Place the meat in the bowl and turn each piece several times to really coat it in the marinade. Cover and let sit for at least 2 hours or up to overnight in the fridge.

About 30 minutes before you want to cook the lamb, light the grill and pull the meat out of the refrigerator. In a small bowl, toss the nectarines with the remaining 1 tablespoon olive oil. When the flames are mostly died down and the coals are glowing red with pale gray ash on the outside, spread the coals, but not too much: You want a pretty hot spot to work with. Place the grate on the grill and, when it is hot, place the lamb on the grill. Grill on one side for 4 to 5 minutes, flip, and cook again on the other side for 4 minutes, or until it reaches 120°F (50°C) for medium rare when measured with an instant-read thermometer.

Let the lamb rest for 10 minutes, then slice along the bias into 1-inch (2.5 cm) slices. Brush the grill, then lay the nectarine pieces on the grate, flesh side down. Cook until sharp grill marks appear, about 3 minutes, then carefully flip each nectarine chunk with a spatula and remove it from the grill. Set them aside. Place the lamb on a serving platter, nestle the nectarine chunks into the meat, and season with flaky salt. Spoon the whipped tahini generously over the meat and drizzle the whole platter with ginger green sauce, if using.

Cocktail makings at home  Beautiful snowy backyard

Wintery crab feast

Oyster Pan Roast with Yuzu Kosho Cream, and Spicy Cornmeal Biscuits

Serves 1 dad, or 2 to 4 ordinary oyster lovers

Like many Northwesterners, my dad loves cooked oysters even more than he loves them fresh, shucked, or raw. He was thrilled when I made this for him, and he ate the whole thing himself, appreciating the citrusy heat of the Japanese hot sauce yuzu kosho alongside the mellow oysters. So, keep in mind the enthusiasm of your dinner guests when figuring out how many oysters to buy! Remember when you are cooking oysters to keep a very light touch with the cooking time—they are best just plumped and frizzled—don't cook them until they shrink down into tough little fists.

For the cornmeal biscuits:

1½ cups (187 g) all-purpose flour

1 cup (120 g) medium-grind cornmeal

1 tablespoon baking powder

½ teaspoon salt

Pinch of cayenne pepper

½ cup (1 stick/115 g) cold unsalted butter, cut into small pieces

1 cup (240 ml) cold heavy cream, plus more as needed

Make the biscuits: Preheat the oven to 350°F (175°C).

In a large bowl, whisk together the flour, cornmeal, baking powder, salt, and cayenne pepper. Using fingers or a pastry blender, cut in the cold butter until the mixture is a mix of pieces from pea-sized lumps to coarse cornmeal–sized bits. Gently stir in the cream. Using your hands, knead together the dough. You might need a touch more cream to get it to a nice cohesive consistency.

Dump out the dough on a lightly floured surface and form a round flat shape. Roll out to 1½ inches (3.8 cm) thick. Using a 2¾- to 3-inch (7 to 7.5 cm) round biscuit cutter, cut out at least 6 biscuits. Reserve any extra dough bits.

Place the biscuits on a sheet pan along with the extra dough bits (to enjoy as a snack) and bake until the biscuits are firm and browning on the edges, 18 to 20 minutes. Remove to a wire rack and let cool. (Whatever is not eaten with the oysters will be delicious for breakfast with butter and honey.)

Make the pan roast: Drain the oysters and reserve their liquor. In a large, heavy skillet, melt the butter over medium heat. Slip in the oysters and cook them halfway, about 2 minutes.

(Recipe continues)

For the pan roast:

1 quart (910 g) shucked yearling oysters, about 24 oysters

3 tablespoons unsalted butter

2 shallots (about 2½ ounces/70 g), thinly sliced into rounds

1 teaspoon chopped thyme leaves

¾ cup (180 ml) white wine, dry white vermouth, or sake

½ cup (120 ml) heavy cream

2 teaspoons green yuzu kosho or other hot sauce

Freshly ground black pepper

Scoop the oysters from the pan to a plate and set aside. Place the pan back over low heat, add the shallots and thyme, and sweat them for about 5 minutes, until they are transparent and begin to brown at the edges. Pour in the wine, turn the heat up to medium-high, and reduce the liquid by half, about 2 minutes. Whisk in the cream and again reduce the liquid by half, about 2 minutes.

Add the oyster liquor and yuzu kosho, bring to a simmer, and simmer for another 3 to 4 minutes. Place the oysters back in the sauce, lower the heat to low, and warm through for about 1 minute.

Serve with freshly cracked black pepper and cornmeal biscuits.

Work in Progress: Personal Meals

Sometimes I love to make a big quantity of a certain dish (see the meatballs on page 220). Other times I like to scale back a bit—an oyster stew or the egg and radicchio scramble (page 147) are so rich and intimate that a more modest portion works well. They are also dishes that are best eaten right away and don't make for great leftovers. When you are thinking about your cooking, keep in mind how you might want to scale your work to suit how you are most likely to enjoy your food.

Rich and Savory Beef Shin with Horseradish and Mint

Serves 4

It took me a minute (and a trip to England) to realize that beef shins were the same cut as osso bucco. Beef shins are always a great deal and deliver so much rich intensity for the investment. It takes a long, slow background braise to cook the meat, but it's almost completely passive—no need to fidget or fuss with the pan. A little bit of anchovy in the pan, along with some lemony coriander seed, helps add complex savory tones to the delicious meat. And I like to serve it with something brisk and fresh, like a shower of freshly grated horseradish and slivered mint leaves. This is great with a simple salad and crusty bread or roasted vegetables.

Note: I like to choose the bigger slices cut from higher on the shin—they give you a better ratio of meat to fat, even if the smaller cuts make cuter individual portions.

4 tablespoons (60 ml) olive oil

4 cloves garlic, shaved with a Microplane

1 teaspoon salt, plus more as needed

½ teaspoon freshly ground black pepper, plus more as needed

1 tablespoon toasted coriander seeds, coarsely ground

Peel of 1 lemon, shaved and sliced into thin ribbons

3 pounds (1.4 kg) beef shin—ask your butcher to cut it into 2 slices (see Note)

2 cups (480 ml) white wine

1 cup (240 ml) tomato puree (passata)

(Ingredients continue)

Combine 2 tablespoons of the olive oil, the garlic, salt, pepper, coriander seeds, and lemon peel in a medium bowl. Whisk well, then massage well into the meat and let sit refrigerated for at least 3 hours or overnight. Remove from the fridge 1 hour before cooking.

Preheat the oven to 350°F (175°C).

In a large Dutch oven, heat the remaining 2 tablespoons olive oil over medium-high heat. Pull out the lemon slivers and set aside. Cook each piece of beef until nicely browned on one side of each slice, then flip and brown the other sides.

Remove the meat from the pan. Pour in the wine and tomato passata and scrape any accumulated browned bits off the bottom of the pan. Stir in the anchovies and let the liquid simmer for 2 minutes. Add the celery and onion and simmer for 2 additional minutes. Add the red chile flakes, rosemary, and the lemon peel from the marinade. Place the meat in the liquid, cover, and place the pan in the oven.

(Recipe continues)

3 anchovy fillets

2 stalks celery, cut into 3-inch (7.5 cm) chunks

1 yellow onion, sliced into 1-inch (2.5 cm) wedges

½ teaspoon red chile flakes

2 (4-inch/10 cm) sprigs rosemary

Flaky salt, to finish

¼ cup (5 g) mint leaves, larger leaves torn

1-inch (2.5 cm) piece fresh horseradish

Roast until the meat is fall-off-the-bone tender and the sauce has thickened and concentrated, about 3½ hours. Remove the rosemary, then transfer the meat and juices to a serving platter. Garnish the meat with flaky salt, then shower with the mint. Generously grate horseradish over the top and serve.

Work in Progress: The Process Is the Point

There is often a short window of intense beauty before food gets properly cooked, and braises are a particular pleasure in that regard. I'll often build my braise in my milk-white enameled Dutch oven. The browned meat is overlaid with colorful aromatics like the lemon peel, rosemary, and chile flakes here—a beautiful and fleeting still life. By the time it's all cooked, its beauty will be more subdued, but I will remember the lovely colors from before. I look for moments to appreciate throughout the cooking process: It's not entirely about the finished product.

My Favorite Desserts

Pass the Soft-Whipped Cream

I'm not the biggest dessert maker—I think I am surrounded by too many people who are completely dedicated to making beautiful sweets, professionally or just as passionate amateurs, to spend too much of my time focusing on baking. But I will say there are times when baking is what I really want to do.

In my last book, *Getaway*, I talked about how important travel is to my creative process. Going away to my favorite places always offers inspiration: I pack my notebooks and camera with ideas to try out at home. But travel also makes me eager to get back to my own kitchen and the creative routines that sustain me through my regular life. When I get home, soon after I drop my bags and get some sleep, I want to restock the kitchen (which I've inevitably emptied before my trip) and cook. More particularly, I find myself wanting to bake. Baking is in some ways the most transformative kind of cooking—you start with the most basic ingredients—flour, sugar, eggs, milk, and then with a little mixing and a little heat, your cakes rise, your cookies crisp, your custards set. It's a way for me to reinvest in the power of the kitchen and to settle back in. And, of course, baking fills the air with sweet aromas and helps me reconnect with the season through its flavors, like summer berries, fall quince, winter citrus, or spring rhubarb. With a slightly more prescriptive nature than savory cooking, baking is like a drawing exercise I turn to to get back in the habit of creating.

So, what kinds of desserts do I feel like making when the fancy strikes me? In general, I want an assertive main character. If it's a berry dessert, I want it to be intensely berried, with just enough sugar to counterbalance the tartness of the summer fruit. I love an eggy custard where the golden yolks are a prominent flavor (and not just a structural necessity). If I'm baking a nutty cookie, I want it to be bumpy and toasted with almost no detectable batter binding together the chunky walnuts. For me, desserts shouldn't pull you in too many different directions: In general, they should be Chocolate. Lemon. Walnut. Not all three. I think the more elements added to a dessert, the less you taste. Elaborate desserts with bits and swirls are not usually interesting or delicious to

me. I want one forkful to communicate all that I am supposed to taste, and I don't want to wonder why something is on the other side of the plate or how I am supposed to eat it.

I chase that kind of clarity in a dessert because I think it creates the strongest responses and most indelible memories. We call my mom Shirlee Pie because she is such a gifted pie-maker and her creations always have that focused intensity: one fruit, in its highest expression, just cradled in a flaky pastry—you'll find her dough method in the recipe for berry crostata (page 246). Berries are still my favorite pie (and crostata) filling because they are so juicy, so messy, so intense.

What else can you say about almost any of my favorite desserts? It will taste good with softly whipped cream or just simple cold cream. This works for almost every pudding, pie, and cookie in this chapter. Cream is that perfect counterpoint to the strong dessert flavors I favor—it is so soft and gentle and in need of a little contrast. You can whip cream with a machine, and occasionally I do, but it's so much lovelier to pour some very cold cream into a bowl and whisk vigorously for a few minutes. Whisk until the cream is fluffy but still runs slowly off the spoon when lifted. With this method it's almost impossible to overwhisk cream so that it tastes like butter, and it's a little burst of activity that can be shared with a helpful dinner guest before dessert is served.

Whipped cream gives a bit of softening diffusion to the intense dessert flavors I'm drawn to, like a bit of leafy shade on a bright summer afternoon. Softness, both in texture and flavor, is an overlooked element in cooking, and my serve-with-cream desserts keep that in mind!

There is one more reason that I'm inclined to bake: when I am craving connection. Part of the particular joy of baking is that it is such a delight to share sweets with others. I'll bring a coffee cake to the office or cut little nibbles of brownie for my niece and nephew. Sweet making gets at that core part of cooking that is about summoning full, happy, uncomplicated feelings.

Shirlee's Brownie, Hold the Nuts

Makes 9 big brownies

My mother, Shirlee, is a great baker and got me hooked on a superior brownie: crisp-edged and fudgy. No soft, cakey brownies for us. And they incorporate a lively mix of cocoa and dark chocolate for maximum chocolate complexity. Brownies are a simple treat, and as I've gotten older, I've jettisoned anything that's not essential. I skip the nuts, which Shirlee loves, unless I have a really stellar batch of new-crop walnuts on hand (see page 243). Why undermine a delicious brownie with blah nuts? I used to add vanilla to everything I baked, but honestly, it's lost amid the chocolate, so I skip that now too. So here is my method— slightly streamlined from Mom's—for a stripped-down, absolutely delicious, classic brownie. I love to serve these with vanilla ice cream or simply on their own with a glass of amaro.

8 ounces (225 g) 70% dark chocolate, broken into small pieces

1 cup (2 sticks/225 g) unsalted butter, cut into 1-inch (2.5 cm) chunks, plus more to grease the pan

4 large eggs, at room temperature

1½ cups (300 g) sugar

½ cup (60 g) all-purpose flour

1 teaspoon sea salt

¼ teaspoon baking powder

¾ cup plus 1 tablespoon (75 g) your best cocoa powder (I like Valrhona), sifted

Preheat the oven to 350°F (175°C). Butter an 8 × 8-inch (20 × 20 cm) square baking pan. Line it with a sheet of parchment paper cut to the width of the pan (it's OK if only two sides of the pan are lined).

Place the chocolate and butter in a heatproof mixing bowl. Set the bowl over a saucepan of gently simmering water, making sure the bottom of the bowl doesn't touch the water. Gently warm just until the chocolate is melted. Remove the bowl from the pan and let cool to lukewarm.

In a stand mixer fitted with a whisk attachment, beat the eggs with the sugar on low speed until combined. Turn the mixer up to high and beat for about 3 minutes, until the mixture is very fluffy and pale and a ribbon trails slowly off the beater when it is lifted up.

In a small bowl, whisk together the flour, salt, baking powder, and cocoa powder.

With the mixer running on low, slowly pour the melted chocolate mixture into the egg mixture, making sure to scrape in every drop of the delicious chocolate mixture. Remove the bowl from the machine, scrape down the sides, and then fold the flour mixture into

(Recipe continues)

the batter with a rubber spatula or wooden spoon. Mix thoroughly, then scrape the batter into the prepared pan and spread evenly across the pan.

Bake for 25 minutes, or until the center doesn't feel wobbly to the touch. The brownies will be puffed when you pull them from the oven and fall as they cool. Don't worry; let them slump. Cool completely before serving. They will firm up once cooled and you will be able to cut them. Cut them into 9 equal squares for big portions or leave them on the counter for everyone to nibble up a slice at a time.

Walnut Brutti ma Buoni Cookies

Makes about 20 cookies

I generally like to eat anything with meringue in it, including cookies. But the idea of making a perfectly symmetrical French macaron is horrifying to me—that's just not the way I cook. (If you bake me macarons, I will gladly eat them, though, I promise!) These very simple cookies take the nuttiness and the chew of a meringue cookie but revel in their own craggy, irregular texture. Somehow all the bumps also allow the sugar in the mix to caramelize in little pockets, adding even more interest to each bit. In Italy, you would most often find these ugly but good cookies made with hazelnuts or almonds. But I love them with walnuts. This might be because I have a particularly good source for the walnuts: One of our cooks at Willmott's Ghost, Mark Kelly, is from a family with a walnut farm in California. Each year, he goes down to claim his personal share of these "brown sugar" walnuts, and he is generous enough to share them with us at the restaurant. This year we brought in 150 pounds of them! They are spectacular. If you don't have a direct hookup with a walnut grower, look for the best ones you can. Often "new-crop" walnuts, available sometime between October and January, are the best. Compared with walnuts that have been sitting in the bulk bins for a mysterious period, they have more sweetness and bright acidity to offset the tannins that make walnuts, well, walnutty. It might be worth the work to shell them yourself. If you nab some great walnuts, eat them within a couple of weeks—with cheese, in salads, or in cookies like these. After that, freeze any extras until you are ready to eat them.

(Recipe continues)

10 ounces (280 g) walnut halves (about 2 cups)

½ teaspoon salt

2 tablespoons natural cocoa powder

3 large egg whites, at room temperature

1 teaspoon lemon juice

1 cup (200 g) sugar

1 teaspoon vanilla extract

Preheat the oven to 350°F (175°C). Line 2 sheet pans with parchment paper.

Spread the walnut halves out on a sheet pan. Place in the oven and toast until slightly golden at their centers, about 8 minutes. (Check often, as different oil levels and humidity in the nuts can cause different toasting times.)

Turn the oven temperature down to 325°F (165°F). Remove the walnuts from the oven and let them cool to room temperature. Place the nuts in a food processor fitted with a metal blade and pulse with the salt and cocoa powder until the nuts have an uneven, rubbly texture: Be careful not to process too finely into a powder.

In a stand mixer outfitted with a whisk, place the egg whites and lemon juice into the bowl. Beat on low speed until the egg whites are foamy. Turn the mixer speed to medium-high and add the sugar a spoonful at a time. Whisk in the vanilla and continue beating until the whites stand in glossy peaks but not until stiff and dry, about 1 minute.

Remove the bowl from the stand and gently fold in the walnut mixture, being careful not to overmix; a few streaks are fine. Spoon the mixture in small, tablespoon-sized heaps onto the prepared sheet pans. Bake the cookies, rotating the pans and reversing them once, until the tops are firm to the touch, about 25 minutes for a chewy cookie. Bake for about 5 minutes more if you want a bit more crunch through and through. Place on a wire rack and cool completely. The cookies can be stored in an airtight container for up to 1 week.

Side-of-the-Road Blackberry Crostata with Shirlee's Piecrust and Soft Whipped Cream

Serves 8

Himalayan blackberries are weeds in our region, but that doesn't stop them from developing delicious fruit in every untended lot, roadside ditch, and eroded hillside around. In blackberry season, all of us Northwesterners are vulnerable to the lure of the brambles. We catch a whiff of hot blackberry juice in the air, or we see how heavy the berries are hanging, and then we become berry-picking zombies—it's impossible to get them all, but that doesn't stop us from trying. We return with fingers stained purple and a few thorny scratches, but with more blackberries than we can actually consume before they turn to mush. So, if you find yourself with an unruly pile of blackberries sitting on your kitchen table (or if you have a similar haul of raspberries), this open-faced tart is one of the lowest-key ways of converting that harvest into a succulent dessert. And if you have spent all your get-up-and-go picking berries and have not a drop of energy left to cook anything, remember that you can freeze your berries on a sheet pan and transfer them to a zip-top bag to bake another day.

2½ cups (315 g) all-purpose flour, plus 1 tablespoon for the filling and more for rolling

1 cup (2 sticks/225 g) cold unsalted butter, cut in 1-inch (2.5 cm) chunks

½ cup (100 g) plus 1 tablespoon sugar

½ teaspoon salt

½ cup (120 ml) icy-cold water

4 cups (about 560 g) blackberries, raspberries, or a mixture

Finely grated zest of 1 lemon

1 tablespoon lemon juice

2 to 3 tablespoons heavy cream, for brushing

Vanilla ice cream or soft whipped cream, to serve

Make the crust: In a food processor, pulse 2½ cups (315 g) of the flour, the butter, 2 teaspoons of the sugar, and the salt until you have a mixture of fine crumbs and pea-sized chunks. Pulse in the cold water until the dough just comes together. Remove the dough from the processor and press it into a large, fat disk. Wrap well and chill for at least 1 hour or up to overnight.

Lightly flour a clean work surface and roll a rolling pin through the flour. Roll the dough out to a large disc that is ¼ inch (6 mm) thick. Lay it on a parchment paper–lined sheet pan and let chill while you prepare the filling.

Preheat the oven to 425°F (220°C).

Make the filling: In a large bowl, combine the berries, the remaining 1 tablespoon flour, ½ cup (100 g) of the remaining sugar, and the lemon zest. I wait to add the

(Recipe continues)

juice until I am ready to put the berries on the dough. It will create juice that will run to the edge and could be messy.

Pull the sheet and dough from the refrigerator. Mix the lemon juice into the berries and then mound the berries on the center of the dough. Leave a 2½- to 3-inch (6 to 7.5 cm) border of dough around the berry pile. Starting in one spot and working clockwise, fold the dough over the berries, pleating every few inches to cinch the dough around the berries. Don't press down too hard onto the fruit or it can crack the dough. Once folded up, put the sheet in the fridge for 30 minutes.

Remove the sheet from the fridge and brush the cream on the dough border. Sprinkle the remaining 1 teaspoon sugar onto the cream. Place the sheet in the oven and bake for 45 to 50 minutes, until the dough is firm and golden brown. Remove from the oven and cool. Serve with vanilla ice cream or soft whipped cream.

Work in Progress: Scaled to Impress

In an earlier sidebar, I mentioned that sometimes a delicate portion is the best choice for a dish, but other times it's fun to make something really monumental. When serving a group, I like to present an impressive pile of a given ingredient. It is so enticing. I will often find a plate that lets me pile my tomato salad or grilled peppers nice and high. With this galette, there is a truly impressive pile of berries before cooking. They cook down during baking, of course, but because of the initial scale, you end up with a loftier crust on the edge and a thicker swath of berries to cut through than if the dessert had been made in a conventional tart pan.

Rhubarb Clafouti for a Big Crowd
(and hopefully leftovers for breakfast)

Serves 8 to 10

French cuisine is known for very fancy desserts, but there is a whole mode of cook-at-home French desserts that are determinedly simple. There is a famous yogurt cake that schoolchildren learn at an early age (traditionally with the yogurt cup as the sole measuring device). This clafouti is another low-effort, high-reward recipe. A clafouti is somewhere between a cake and a custard. I love an eggy custard. It's perfect for celebrating seasonal fruit, and it isn't easy as pie, it's easier. Most traditional clafouti made in France uses unpitted cherries, but I have been to the dentist one too many times to continue that tradition. These days, I whip it up with frozen sour cherries (pitted!), frozen raspberries, or tart nectarines. Any fruit with sourness that verges on insolence is a good candidate for the softening effect of a clafouti. And, so, my favorite variation is here, the perfect way to welcome one of the first sharp tastes of spring to hit the market—rhubarb, particularly the hibiscus-pink forced rhubarb that shows up around Valentine's Day in the Northwest. For a little extra drama, I like to keep the spears long instead of cutting them into more convenient but less dramatic chunks.

Butter, to grease

1½ cups (300 g) sugar, plus a bit more for the pan

6 large eggs

1 cup (240 ml) milk

1½ cups (360 ml) sour cream

2 teaspoons vanilla extract

¾ teaspoon salt

1 cup (125 g) all-purpose flour

10 stalks rhubarb, about 8 inches (20 cm) long

Cold heavy cream, to serve

Preheat the oven to 375°F (190°C). Butter and sugar a large gratin dish (16 × 11 inches/40 × 28 cm) or 2 pie dishes.

In a blender, combine the eggs, 1¼ cups (250 g) of the sugar, the milk, sour cream, vanilla, and salt. Blend at top speed until smooth. Add the flour and blend on high speed for about 1 minute to make it very frothy. Pour the mixture into the prepared pan(s), then arrange the rhubarb on top in parallel lines, with the shorter spears on the outside.

Sprinkle the top with the remaining ¼ cup (50 g) sugar and bake for 40 minutes. The clafouti is done when it springs back a bit when poked gently in the middle. If the recipe is divided into two pans, it will cook faster. Return to the oven for about 5 more minutes if the custard is not set. Cool for 10 minutes and serve warm, scooped into low bowls with cold cream poured over the top.

Roasted Plum Ice Cream

Makes 2 quarts (2 liters)

If you can get your hands on Hollywood or Santa Rosa plums, get ready for an incredibly striking magenta-toned ice cream. It tastes as vivid as it looks with plenty of tang from the sweet-tart plums all cushioned by a rich, eggy French custard. The plush texture and decadence are so nostalgic for me.

Ice cream making has always been almost as rewarding for me as eating it. In long-ago summers, my brother and I would be sent to the back deck on hand-cranked churning duty to help make my mom's strawberry ice cream, cranking and cranking and shoveling in more ice and rock salt as it melted through the slats of the barrel. These days, my little portable ice cream maker takes considerably less mess and work. This gorgeous ice cream would, of course, be nice with shortbread or a slice of plain almond cake, but I also argue for the ice cream as its own proud dessert. It doesn't always have to be a condiment for other sweets.

2 pounds (900 g) fresh plums, preferably red-fleshed ones like Hollywood or Santa Rosa

½ teaspoon salt

6 large egg yolks

¾ cup (165 g) brown sugar

2 cups (480 ml) heavy cream

1 vanilla bean, scraped, or 2 teaspoons vanilla extract

2 tablespoons Goslings dark rum or vodka

Preheat the oven to 425°F (220°C). Line a sheet pan with parchment paper.

Halve the plums and place them skin side down on the prepared sheetpan. Roast until the plums start to collapse and the juice starts to spill out, 15 to 18 minutes. Remove from the oven and set aside to cool. Place the plums and salt in a blender and buzz on high speed until smooth.

In the bowl of a stand mixer fitted with a whisk, beat the egg yolks and ½ cup (110 g) of the brown sugar until the mixture has doubled in size and is pale yellow and ribbony in texture.

Have ready a large bowl filled halfway with ice water and a second metal bowl of similar size that will fit in the first without sinking into the water. In a large heavy-bottomed saucepan, heat the cream with the remaining ¼ cup (55 g) brown sugar and the vanilla pod, if using, over medium heat until it gets very steamy (just short of boiling). Pour the cream into a large measuring cup or pitcher. With the stand mixer running on low, slowly—very slowly—drizzle the

(Recipe continues)

252

scalded milk into the egg mixture. Be very careful with this step; do not rush it or the egg yolks will cook and curdle, ruining the custard.

Once the egg yolks and cream are mixed, return the mixture to the saucepan. Cook over medium heat, slowly stirring constantly with a rubber spatula until the custard thickens significantly (175°F/80°C max). Quickly strain the custard through a fine sieve into the metal bowl. Whisk in the plum puree, vanilla extract, if using, and rum. Place the bowl into the ice water bath and stir until the custard reaches room temperature.

Once cool, cover and chill the custard for at least 2 hours in the fridge—overnight is great. Spin the ice cream as your maker suggests; depending on the size of your maker, you may need to freeze the custard in two batches. Serve right away for soft serve, or pack into a chilled container and freeze for a few hours for a firmer texture.

Work in Progress: Playing with Temperature

Temperature is another creative tool in the kitchen that can have a big impact on a dish. Even ice cream can be served well tempered and slightly puddly or balled up in firm scoops. There's a full range of temperatures beyond hot and cold—you can have piping hot soup to delicately spoon up or a gently warm oyster stew. I usually like my butter room temperature for spreading on toast, but if I am serving a little canape with, say, an anchovy on top of a slice of bread, I like to use a firm platform of cold butter shaved into a little ribbon—it's the same ingredient but a different effect. As a practical tip, think about the temperature of your serving dish—serving cold salad on a dishwasher-warm plate can defeat some of your purposes, as can hot risotto in a chilly bowl.

Our hollywood Plum harvest

floppy tulips & rhubarb

Island flowers

Poached Bosc Pears with Rosemary, Orange Peel, and Vanilla Bean

Serves 6 to 8

When summer ends and autumn dusk starts to fall in the midafternoon, it can be hard to say goodbye to the warm weather. But there are special moments that can only happen as the weather chills and the rain comes to the Pacific Northwest. The sunlight slicing beneath the cloud ceiling to light up the autumn leaves, the return of local oysters to their best season, and the possibility of eating a perfectly ripe Bosc pear. Other pear varieties are wonderful but can be hard to catch at peak ripeness before they descend into mush. Bosc pears don't give in so quickly and keep a chilly, crisp, pleasingly granular texture. They are so good sliced into salads, but I also love them poached, which can make a good pear turn angelic. My mother would poach pears from our backyard very simply, in simple sugar syrup. I would gobble up the sweet, slithery fruit with cottage cheese and a shower of black pepper (don't knock it until you've tried it!). When I make mine now, I still like a hint of something savory alongside the honey-sweet pears, so I add a couple of sprigs of garden rosemary to my wine-based syrup, alongside vanilla bean and orange peel. I'll serve those delicious pears with crème fraîche (or ice cream if the mood strikes). Any leftovers make a lovely breakfast atop some oatmeal or, you know, with some cottage cheese and black pepper!

(Recipe continues)

4 cups (960 ml) white wine

1⅓ cups (265 g) sugar

Zest of 1 orange, cut into long strips

1 vanilla bean, split

2 large sprigs rosemary
(6 to 8 inches/15 to 20 cm long)

5 Bosc pears, peeled and halved
(about 2 pounds/910 g)

Crème fraîche, to serve

Adjust a rack to the lower third of the oven and pre-heat the oven to 400°F (205°C).

In a large, nonreactive saucepan or Dutch oven, heat the wine and sugar over medium heat, stirring until the sugar dissolves. Add the orange peel, vanilla bean, and rosemary and cook for about another couple of minutes, until the liquid is at a low simmer. Slide the pears into the liquid and cover, if desired, with a cartouche (a piece of parchment paper the diameter of the pot), pressing the paper onto the surface of the liquid.

Place the pan in the oven and cook the pears, occasionally lifting the parchment and spooning the syrup over the topmost pears. You will also need to gently flip each pear a couple of times during baking. Work gently, as the pot and syrup will be hot and the pears become quite tender as they cook. The pears are done when a small knife easily slips into them, about 1½ hours.

Remove the pears from the oven and cool to room temperature, then place the pears and syrup into an airtight container in the fridge, where they will keep nicely for up to 3 days. Serve chilled with a spoonful of crème fraîche beside each pear.

Sourdough Bread Pudding with Huckleberries and Hard Sauce

Serves 8 to 10

Huckleberries are found clinging to woodland shrubs from late summer well into fall—there are a few varieties, but they are all tart and savory-sweet—a real wild fruit. I'll pick a few when I go hiking, but it takes a lot of effort to get any real baking amount of them. I'm grateful to purveyors like Foraged and Found who bring the taste of the mountains to me. Even if you don't live in huckleberry country, they can reliably get frozen berries shipped to you with an online order. If that's too much, try making my favorite version of bread pudding with another tart berry (I'd take raspberries over blueberries, for example). This recipe works in a gratin dish, but I like to make the dessert in two pie dishes, so I can bring one to each end of the table and let my guests scoop out their own portions of the pudding. Then they can pour in cold cream, and for a little bit of extra muchness, a scoop of sweet boozy hard sauce, essentially a thick, buttery glaze. If you're serving for brunch and not dessert, you might skip the sugary sauce and just serve the cream—I will leave it up to you.

(Recipe continues)

3 large eggs

4 cups (960 ml) heavy cream

1½ cups (300 g) sugar

¾ teaspoon salt

1 teaspoon almond extract

1 pound (455 g) loaf sourdough bread, ripped apart into roughly 1-inch (2.5 cm) pieces (don't cut it, if you can avoid it)

Butter, to grease the pans

2½ cups (340 g) frozen wild huckleberries or raspberries

Cold heavy cream, to serve

Bonus Hard Sauce (recipe follows; optional)

Place a rack in the center of the oven and preheat the oven to 350°F (175°C).

In a large bowl, whisk the eggs until blended. Add the cream, sugar, salt, and almond extract and whisk thoroughly. When well blended, fold in the bread chunks. Push the bread into the liquid, then cover and refrigerate for at least 30 minutes or up to overnight.

Generously butter 2 (9-inch/23 cm) pie plates or 1 large baking dish (9 × 13 inches/23 × 33 cm).

When ready to bake, fold the frozen berries into the bread mixture. Divide evenly between the 2 pans (or place in the single baking dish). Place the dishes/dish on a sheet pan and bake for 45 minutes to 1 hour until the custard is set and the peaks of the bread are toasty brown.

If the bread pudding cools to room temperature, reheat it for 8 to 10 minutes before serving. (You can do this in the original baking dish, or if you're just serving a couple of people, scoop out individual portions and reheat in ovenproof serving dishes.)

Serve the pudding warm with cold cream poured on top and, if you like, warm bonus hard sauce.

Bonus Hard Sauce

Makes about 2¼ cups (510 ml)

½ cup (1 stick/115 g) unsalted butter

2 cups sifted confectioners' sugar

½ teaspoon salt

½ cup (120 ml) bourbon

1 (14-ounce/400 g) can sweetened condensed milk

In a medium saucepan, melt the butter over low heat. Whisk in the confectioners' sugar and salt until they have mostly dissolved into the butter; it may seize a bit, but don't worry. Pull the pan off the heat and stir in the bourbon, which will smooth out the mixture. Return to the heat and simmer for another 5 minutes. Whisk in the condensed milk. Once thoroughly blended, set aside. Serve warm. Store in an airtight container in the refrigerator for up to 1 week.

Carla Leonardi's Rice Pudding Cake and Orange Crema Inglese

Serves 8 to 10

Carla Leonardi has been an inspiration for me for a long time: She founded Café Lago in 1990, and it has been a Seattle constant for elegant, delicious, and straightforward Italian food ever since. When I first started working with food, it was exciting to see a woman working the pizza oven at a busy place like Lago—women in the kitchen were even rarer then than now, and she helped show me the path. Carla also has an infectious generosity—and sharing this recipe with me is just one example. This cake is just the kind of homey but special dessert I love the best: a rice pudding with a sliceable shape and an amber halo of caramel for a bit of lushness. I love each chilly mouthful of this dessert, and it is so good served with a blob of softly whipped cream and whatever juicy fruits are in season. If you have a little more time, you can also make orange crema inglese, the sweet custard sauce boosted with fancy orange essential oil, to make everything even more voluptuous. The other great thing about this dessert (including the crema) is that it is easiest made the day before serving, so you can scratch it off your list ahead of time.

⅓ cup (50 g) golden raisins

¼ cup (60 ml) dark rum or brandy

6 cups (1.4 liters) whole milk

1 cup (190 g) Arborio rice

1½ cups (300 g) plus 1 tablespoon sugar

1 teaspoon salt

1 vanilla bean, split

4 large eggs, separated

Soft whipped cream or Orange Crema Inglese (recipe follows), to serve (optional)

Fresh seasonal fruit (optional)

In a small bowl, soak the raisins in the rum for 1 hour.

In a heavy-bottomed medium saucepan, combine the milk, rice, ½ cup (100 g) of the sugar, the salt, and split vanilla bean. Bring to a boil over medium heat, then turn the heat down to medium-low to maintain a simmer. Cover the pan and cook, stirring occasionally, for 30 minutes. Remove the lid and keep cooking and stirring for another 20 minutes, for 50 minutes total, or until the rice absorbs all the liquid. Remove from the heat, scrape the remaining seeds from the vanilla bean into the pudding, and discard the pod. Set the rice aside to cool to room temperature.

Place a rack at the center of the oven with nothing above it and preheat the oven to 375°F (190°C).

Cover the outside of a 9-inch (23 cm) springform pan with one or two layers of aluminum foil (so that water

(Recipe continues)

from the water bath you'll make later will not seep into the pan). Have ready a shallow baking dish into which the pan fits comfortably.

Pour the remaining 1 cup (200 g) sugar into a heavy, dry skillet and shake so the sugar spreads evenly. Place over medium-high heat so the sugar begins to melt without stirring. After about 2 minutes, stir with a wooden spoon until the sugar is dark amber and just beginning to foam, about 3 minutes. Working quickly so the sugar doesn't harden, remove from the heat and carefully pour the sugar into the prepared springform pan, tipping the pan to coat the bottom and sides as best as possible. Drain the raisins and discard the rum. Stir the egg yolks and raisins into the cooled rice.

Using a stand mixer fitted with a whisk, beat the egg whites on high until foamy, then add the remaining 1 tablespoon sugar and beat until soft peaks form. Fold the fluffy whites into the rice mixture.

Pour the rice mixture into the caramelized sugar-coated springform pan and set the pan in the shallow baking dish. Place the baking dish on the rack in the oven. Pour hot tap water into the baking dish, letting it come about halfway up the sides of the pan. Bake until a knife inserted into the middle comes out clean, about 1 hour and 15 minutes. Remove from the water bath and let cool. Remove the springform ring around the pan, and gently place a serving plate on top of the cake. Invert the cake onto the plate. Let cool to room temperature, then refrigerate for at least 2 hours before serving chilled with soft whipped cream or orange crema inglese, if using.

Orange Crema Inglese

Makes about 2½ cups (600 ml)

2 cups (480 ml) heavy cream

5 tablespoons (63 g) sugar

2 (2-inch/5 cm) orange strips, no pith please

5 large egg yolks

Boyajian pure orange oil (optional)

Gently warm the cream and sugar in a small saucepan over medium-low heat until the sugar is dissolved and a few bubbles start to rise at the edge of the pan. Remove from the heat, then add the orange strips, cover, and let infuse for about 1 hour.

Make an ice bath in a large bowl and rest a smaller metal bowl on top of the ice.

Whisk the yolks in a separate bowl. Re-warm the cream mixture to a bare simmer. Slowly pour 1 cup (240 ml) of the cream mixture into the egg yolks, whisking constantly as you pour.

Pour the warm cream and egg mixture back into the saucepan and cook over medium heat, stirring constantly with a heatproof spatula, until the cream coats it. Strain the custard through a fine sieve into the bowl set over ice. Press any remaining flavor from the orange peels and discard them. Stir in a few drops of the orange oil, to taste, if using. Stir until cooled. Serve alongside the rice pudding cake (or with the poached pear or the brownie!).

Lemon Posset with Raspberry Compote and Thyme

Serves 4

Possets emerged in England as a curative food—warm, thickened, sometimes sweetened milk to restore the strength of an invalid. This more contemporary version of a posset is more about soothing your taste buds with creaminess and restoring them with a bright lemon zing. The most wonderful part of this dessert is that it can be made the day of a dinner party with almost no effort. A little dollop of raspberry compote makes a pretty contrast in flavor and color. Cookies are nice too!

2 cups (480 ml) heavy cream

1½ teaspoons salt

8 sprigs thyme

⅔ cup (135 g) sugar

¼ cup (60 ml) lemon juice

Raspberry Compote (recipe follows) or your favorite jam, to serve

Red or black cap raspberries to garnish, optional

In a medium saucepan, combine the cream, salt, thyme, and sugar. Place over medium heat and whisk until the sugar is dissolved and the mixture comes to a boil. Cook at a controlled boil for 5 minutes, standing watch and stirring occasionally to make sure the mixture does not scorch or boil over. Remove from the heat and stir in the lemon juice. Let sit for about 10 minutes. Strain through a fine sieve, and then pour into the prettiest little clear glass cups you have and set in the fridge for at least 2 hours or up to 2 days. Cover the possets with a bit of plastic wrap once they have cooled. Serve with a spot of raspberry compote or your favorite jam, and garnish with raspberries if desired.

Raspberry Compote

Makes 2¼ cups (540 ml)

4½ cups (565 g) raspberries, fresh or frozen (I use frozen because I crave this in the winter, but frozen is great year-round)

¼ cup (50 g) sugar

2 tablespoons lemon juice

Pinch of salt

Combine all the ingredients in a small saucepan, bring to a simmer over medium heat, and simmer for 1 to 2 minutes, then give it a stir with a wooden spoon. Keep simmering for another 2 to 3 minutes, stirring often. Then turn it up a bit to get the mixture to a soft boil for another 2 minutes, to thicken it just a touch. You want it to be a loose sauce, not like jam. Let cool and serve with all your favorites, including this posset. If you have any leftovers, it is delicious on cornmeal waffles too. Store leftover compote in an airtight container in the refrigerator for up to 1 week or a couple of months in the freezer.

Say yes to champagne

Raspberries from Mom & Dad

Summer flowers in the Skagit Valley

Raspberry and Pecan Crumble Cake

Serves 8

I love all things Diana Henry, the famed British food writer—and a friend of mine!—whose books are packed with recipes that are the perfect blend of elegance and ease. This cake is a take on her rhubarb and almond cake, which is my very favorite kind of cake—one that is casual enough for breakfast or midafternoon snacking but also fancy enough for a dinner-party dessert. It's sweet, but not too much, with a wonderful, generous layer of streusel. The raspberries add a layer of gentle sharpness to balance the buttery richness. This cake is delicious with cream whipped into lazy, soft peaks. But I also adore it with ice cream that's been generously tempered to an almost soft-serve texture. Of course, you could lean away from dessert and toward snacking and serve the cake with a bracing pot of coffee, in which case you don't need the whipped cream.

For the cake:

¾ cup (1½ sticks/170 g) unsalted butter, plus a bit more to butter the pan, softened

¾ cup (150 g) sugar

3 large eggs, at room temperature

½ teaspoon salt

1 teaspoon vanilla extract

1 cup (125 g) all-purpose flour, sifted

1 teaspoon baking powder

2 tablespoons milk

2½ cups (300 g) raspberries, fresh or frozen

(Ingredients continue)

Make the cake: Preheat the oven to 350°F (175°C). Butter a 9-inch (23 cm) springform pan and line the bottom with a circle of parchment paper. Butter the paper as well.

In a stand mixer fitted with a paddle, beat the butter and ½ cup (100 g) of the sugar on low speed to combine, then continue on medium-high speed until the mixture is pale, soft, and fluffy, about 2 minutes. With the mixer on low speed, add the eggs one at a time, stopping to scrape down the sides after each addition. The batter will curdle at this point. Don't worry. Mix in the salt and vanilla and scrape again. Turn off the machine and add the flour and baking powder, then mix on low speed until barely combined. Thin the batter out by mixing in the milk, then pour the batter into the prepared pan.

In a small bowl, toss the raspberries with the remaining ¼ cup (50 g) sugar and arrange them evenly on top of the cake batter.

Make the crumble: In a medium bowl, combine the flour and brown sugar. Toss in the cold butter pieces and press and smoosh the butter into the flour

(Recipe continues)

For the crumble:

1½ cups (190 g) all-purpose flour

⅓ cup (60 g) brown sugar

½ cup (1 stick/115 g) cold unsalted butter, cut into small pieces

1½ cups (160 g) whole pecans, roughly chopped

For serving:

Soft whipped cream, ice cream, or crème fraîche (optional)

mixture by hand, working the butter to break down into small pea-sized pieces (this crumble is rather loose compared to some other coffee cake streusels, but it cooks into a beautiful crackly crust). When mixed well, toss in the pecans and stir well. Sprinkle the crumble mixture onto the raspberry layer. Spread out the mixture just a bit, but don't try to make it flat. The unevenness will make it better.

Bake until a skewer poked into the center of the cake emerges clean and the topping is lovely and brown, 70 to 80 minutes. Let the cake cool on a wire rack for 15 minutes before running a knife around the sides and removing the springform ring. Let cool completely and serve with soft whipped cream, ice cream, or crème fraîche, if using.

Tiramisu in Good Company

Serves 8 to 10

We are all allowed to say we love tiramisu again. After a decade of ubiquity around the turn of the century, it was deemed a little played out. Tiramisu lovers had to quietly spoon up their favorite dessert. But how could something as classic as coffee-soaked biscuits layered with whipped mascarpone really go out of fashion? It's as timeless as it gets. So my recipe doesn't vary much from tradition, but I think the quality of your cocoa, coffee, and alcohol all matter to the resulting deliciousness of the dessert.

I do mess around with how I build the dessert, and I hope you might do so as well: pudding cups for individual portions, low bowls to serve smaller groups, or a gorgeous clear trifle bowl. If you want to consolidate the recipe, you can also use a more traditional ceramic baking dish like a deep-dish lasagna pan for this recipe. The key with a tiramisu dish is making sure it has some depth. The recipe here will serve a big group, because I think tiramisu is more fun in a crowd. If you want to make one for personal use, don't worry—the recipe scales down easily. Have fun with the decision.

(Recipe continues)

For the coffee mixture:

3 cups (720 ml) super-strong brewed coffee or espresso

3 tablespoons sugar

3 tablespoons booze (Marsala is classic, but good rum is delicious too)

For the cream mixture:

8 large egg yolks

1 cup (200 g) sugar

1½ cups (360 ml) heavy cream

1 pound (455 g) mascarpone cheese

To assemble:

⅓ cup (30 g) unsweetened cocoa powder, for dusting

1 package ladyfingers, about 14 ounces (400 g)

Make the coffee mixture: In a medium bowl, whisk together the coffee, sugar, and your booze of choice.

Make the cream mixture: It's easiest to use handheld beaters for this process, since you are whipping two different bowlfuls separately before combining, but you can also use a stand mixer outfitted with a whisk and transfer at each stage.

First, whisk the egg yolks with half of the sugar until the mixture is pale yellow and holds a ribbony shape when the beaters are lifted. Set it aside.

In another large mixing bowl, beat the heavy cream until frothy. Pour in the remaining sugar and whip until soft peaks form.

Fold the mascarpone into the cream, then beat on medium speed to form medium-soft peaks. Gently fold the mascarpone mixture into the egg mixture.

To assemble the tiramisu: Have ready a small sieve set over a bowl. Put the cocoa into the sieve and keep it nearby. One at a time, dip each ladyfinger into the coffee mixture and fill in the bottom of your chosen container—a lasagna pan (13½ × 9¼ × 3¼ inches/34 × 23 × 9 cm) or a tiramisu dish at least 3 inches (7.5 cm) deep—with a layer of the dipped cookies.

Next, spread a layer about ½ inch (12 mm) thick of the cream mixture over the cookie layer. Dust the cream layer from edge to edge with an even layer of cocoa powder. Repeat the layering process to fill your container, finishing with a layer of cream and a dusting of cocoa powder. Let the tiramisu sit for at least 1 hour or cover snugly and refrigerate overnight.

If I am presenting it in its container (rather than scooping out portions), I tend to wait to put the final cream and cocoa layer on until I serve it, so the cocoa keeps its lovely, even, velvety color.

Acknowledgments

Thank you, Thank you!

This story, the one that connects my creative lives, art, and cooking, started a long time ago. I was ten years old when my parents signed me up for a drawing class, where I learned how to draw with pastels on velvet paper. I chose to draw a snow leopard. It was just the head, and the leopard was made up of smudges of grays on a gray background. Oddly, it's something that I still love to this day. Maybe because it was the first thing that was framed and put up on our walls, or because forty-plus years later it's still something I am very proud of. This class was just the beginning of my life made better by art.

Mom and Dad, thank you for always supporting my creative desires. From my first drawing class to encouraging me into a painting degree and on to owning my first restaurant, Boat Street Café. I know how fortunate I am to have your ongoing love and support. The opportunity to think about life visually, creatively, and culinarily is so rewarding and delicious. I love you.

Making this book has been a brilliant challenge to honor creativity in all its forms. My love for painting, and now photography, has been a lifelong lesson from so many creative giants in my life. Thank you to Gail Barnfather, Lynn Saad, Jeffry Mitchell, Curtis Steiner, Ellen Lesperance, Michael Spafford, and Jamie Walker.

Of course this is a book of recipes and stories, and there are so many people in my culinary world who have inspired and taught me. Many I have met only inside their books. Thank you, Diana Henry, Emiko Davies, Margot Henderson, Nigel Slater, Sarit Packer and Itamar Srulovich, Claudia Rodin, Patience Gray, Skye Gyngell, Anissa Helou, Spencer and Sabrina Bezaire, Sarah Grueneberg, Jeremy Sewall, Stuart Brioza, Nicole Krasinski, Dano Sanchez, Aaron and Stacy Franklin, Juan Cassalett, Jill Mathias. Chef Camp Forever!

So much of what inspires me is travel. Thank you to my always ready-to-fly group of friends, Carrie Omegna, Christine Hammond, Margaret Edwins, Lara Hamilton, Nicole Hernandez, Katherine Miller, Irene Wong.

A giant thank-you to all the Sea Creatures teams at our restaurants here in Seattle. Writing a book removes me from the restaurants, but thanks to you, all is well. Your care and craft of making food and dining experiences is incredible. A special thank-you to Bobby Palmquist, Alexa Dallas, Bryant Peng, Jen O'Neil, Brittany Walker, and Lidia de Bernardo, for literally taking care of the business, and to my crazy and perfect business partners, Jeremy Price, Chad Dale, and Ira Gerlich.

Special thanks to Eric Tra, DJTRAMA, for assisting me on the photos in this book, helping me edit everything, and taking late-night calls when I can't seem to find photos in Dropbox. Hero!

Thank you, Bernie Alonzo and Christy Erickson, for the huge Dungeness crab haul and the gorgeous days shooting at your home in Edison, Washington. Can't wait to be neighbors.

Thank you to our Hama Hama Oyster Co. family. No surprise here . . . you're my favorite. Always will be.

Thank you to Katie and Amy at Bitters Co. for the lovely spot to host my book party!

Thank you in abundance to my agent, Katherine Cowles; your calm, kind focus, and persistence were very much needed and appreciated.

The team at Abrams, including my editor, Laura Dozier. It never is an easy ride making a book, and I thank you for letting me push back A LOT on all the things. Grateful for your patience with me moving through this project.

Thank you to my brother, Ryan, and his lovely kids, Maggie and Mateo, for being great assistants and helping with all the weird tasks, including early-morning shrimping runs and doing dishes!

Big love to you, Sara Dickerman. This book could not have happened without you. Thank you for sifting through all the crazy ideas and translating them into beautiful words. You're truly the best.

Finally, a very sweet thank-you to my husband, Dan Crookston, who supported all the madness that is writing, cooking, shooting, and painting a cookbook in our home in Seattle. I love you.

Index

Note: Page numbers in *italics* indicate photos.

Editor: Laura Dozier
Designer: Jeremy Price
Design Managers: Danielle Youngsmith
  and Zach Bokhour
Managing Editor: Lisa Silverman
Production Manager: Kathleen Gaffney

Library of Congress Control Number:
2024931533

ISBN: 978-1-4197-4040-4
eISBN: 978-1-64700-259-6

Printed and bound in China
10 9 8 7 6 5 4 3 2 1

Abrams books are available at special discounts
when purchased in quantity for premiums and pro-
motions as well as fundraising or educational use.
Special editions can also be created to specification.
For details, contact specialsales@abramsbooks.com
or the address below.

Abrams® is a registered trademark of
Harry N. Abrams, Inc.

ABRAMS The Art of Books
195 Broadway, New York, NY 10007
abramsbooks.com

Renee Erickson is the James Beard Award–winning chef and co-owner of numerous Seattle restaurants, including the Walrus and the Carpenter, Willmott's Ghost, and Lioness. She is the author of *Getaway: Food & Drink to Transport You* and *A Boat, a Whale & a Walrus: Menus and Stories*.

Sara Dickerman is a James Beard Award–winning food writer and the author of several cookbooks.